13

VERY SURPRISING
SAYINGS
and Why Jesus Said Them

DAVID C COOK

transforming lives together

13 VERY SURPRISING SAYINGS AND WHY JESUS SAID THEM
Published by David C Cook
4050 Lee Vance Drive
Colorado Springs, CO 80918 U.S.A.

David C Cook U.K., Kingsway Communications
Eastbourne, East Sussex BN23 6NT, England

The graphic circle C logo is a registered trademark of David C Cook.

All Scripture quotations are taken from the *Holy Bible*, New Living Translation, copyright © 1996, 2007 by Tyndale House Foundation. Used by permission of Tyndale House Publishers, Inc., Carol Stream, Illinois 60188. All rights reserved.

LCCN 2017952579
ISBN 978-1-4347-1255-4
eISBN 978-0-8307-7297-1

© 2018 David C Cook

The Team: Lindsay Black, Amy Konyndyk, Rachael Stevenson,
Lu Ann J. Nickelson, Abby DeBenedittis, Susan Murdock
Cover Illustration/Design: Dennis Jones

Printed in the United States of America
First Edition 2018

1 2 3 4 5 6 7 8 9 10

111517

"Midway through the festival, Jesus went up to the Temple and began to teach. The people were surprised when they heard him."

John 7:14-15

Contents

How to Use These
Sessions

About These Sessions

First, thanks. Thanks for caring about children and for helping them explore the surprising things Jesus said. Because Jesus did say some surprising stuff—stuff that left even his closest friends scratching their heads, wondering if he was serious. The first will be *last*? Start fishing for *people*? Love your *enemies*? Really?

And if some of what Jesus said confuses grown-ups, imagine how confusing it sounds to children. Well, no more. You're about to help kids discover the faith-building, life-changing truths tucked into some of Jesus's most surprising sayings.

Welcome to Easy

These sessions for elementary kids are carefully designed to make your life easier. They're light on supplies, quick to prepare, and long on fun. You'll find most supplies in the church's supply closet or kitchen or at home in your garage, pantry, or junk drawer—no need to spend time ordering materials online.

Because these sessions are created so beginning teachers or mature teenagers can lead them confidently, you won't need highly trained teachers. And the variety of options in each session will snag the attention—and hold it—of first-grade through sixth-grade children, including the boys!

Best of all, you'll see kids grow in their faith as they open their hearts to what God shares with them through these 13 sessions.

Welcome to Simple Learning

Preparation is easy too. Each session, you'll focus on one key Bible truth, which children will explore and apply. You'll drive that point home through Bible exploration, fun discussions, giggle-worthy games, and "Oh, wow!" activities that engage kids in multiple ways through multiple learning styles.

Welcome to Deep Bible Discovery

Each week, your children will actually *experience* a Bible truth. They'll discover it, ponder it, talk about it, pray about it, and apply what they learn. If that's what you're looking for—for your children to *do* God's Word instead of just hear it—you're in exactly the right place. And here's a tip: supersize the learning by using a kid-friendly version of the Bible to make sure Jesus's words are understood by children.

Welcome to Flexibility

We get it: sometimes, you have to punt. A sermon goes long … or short. Kids are quick to dive into a lesson or need some time to warm up to being together. Older kids might zip through an activity while their younger friends take a little longer.

Relax. We've got you covered.

You can use these sessions with kids in practically any setting: in Sunday school, children's church, evening programs, or while kids' parents are attending an adult class or small group. There's maximum flexibility because each session is written to last 45 minutes and then provides enough extras to fill a full hour. These sessions stretch to fit exactly what you need, when you need it. They're …

- **multi-aged**—suitable for mixed ages of elementary children;
- **easily adapted**—sessions work for just a couple kids or a packed classroom;
- **relational**—children grow close to Jesus *and* one another;
- **flexible**—brimming with options to fit varying time frames; and
- **fun**—even easily distracted kids will engage, learn, and grow.

So are you ready for some fun? Let's dive in!

Jesus Said ...

Love Your Enemies

The Point: Love everyone—even the meanies!
Scripture Connect: Matthew 5:43–47

Supplies for all session 1 activities options: colored paper plates, flour or clean sand (½ cup per child), table, plastic cups (1 per child, plus a few more), stopwatch, Bible, scraps of paper, pen, container (bowl, box, basket, or paper bag), index cards (1 per child), pencils

The Basics for Leaders

Ask your kids if they have enemies, and they may answer with puzzled looks. That's because *enemies* isn't a word kids tend to use. But ask about bullies or mean kids, and you'll discover that kids' worlds are full of enemies.

That was true of Jesus's world too. There was no shortage of bullies in his life, of people who wished him harm. Yet Jesus told his followers to not just tolerate enemies but to actually *love* them. To *pray* for them.

And Jesus didn't just talk about loving enemies; he showed us how that surprising way of treating enemies looks when lived out. As you share this session with your kids, you'll help them discover that they too can love everyone—even the meanies!

OPENING ACTIVITY–OPTION 1

TELL ME THUMBTHING
Time: about 5 minutes, depending on attendance
Supplies: none

After the kids arrive, say: **When people like a movie, they sometimes give it a thumbs-up.** (demonstrate) **If they really like the movie, they give it two thumbs-up. If they dislike or really dislike the movie, they give it one or two thumbs-down.** (demonstrate)

Say: **Please rate how this past week has gone for you. Was it a one or two thumbs-up week? A one or two thumbs-down week? Or maybe you'd give it one thumbs-up and one thumbs-down—it was a good** *and* **bad week. Rate your week now.**

After kids rate their weeks, give them 30 seconds each to explain why they rated their weeks as they did. You'll go first, sharing a story that models the sort of brief, personal stories you hope kids will share too.

Children will express themselves more over time, and hearing their stories will help you adapt this session to make it even more relevant to your kids' lives.

OPENING ACTIVITY–OPTION 2

ENEMY PLATES

Time: about 10 minutes
Supplies: colored paper plates (1 per child), flour or clean sand (½ cup per child)
Note: If any of the kids have gluten allergies, substitute clean sand for flour.

Give each child a paper plate. Ask the children to place their plates on a level, flat surface such as a tabletop or the floor. Place about a half cup of flour on each plate. Ask kids to carefully spread out the flour on their plates by *gently* brushing it around with their fingers. Then show them how to create a sketch by using your index finger to move the flour around.

Say: **I want you to sketch someone who has bullied you. Someone who has been mean to you in the past or maybe is being mean to you now. Get sketching!** Allow kids time to draw, then say: **Look at your sketch and think about that bully. Think about how it felt when that bully laughed at you or made you feel small and helpless.**

Say: **Call out words that describe how you felt when you were being bullied.** Then tell kids to "erase" their sketches by gently brushing the flour around on their plates with their fingers to redistribute it. Then ask the kids to sketch how they felt when they were being bullied.

After the children are finished sketching, announce that it's show-and-tell time. Ask them to take turns showing what they sketched and—without mentioning their bully's name—telling how what they drew reflects how they felt. After that, have them each draw a heart on their plates.

Say: **This heart is what Jesus would draw if you asked him how he felt about bullies in his life. There were lots of bullies and enemies who made fun of Jesus and hurt him. Jesus says we are to love** *our* **enemies in the same way he loves** *his* **enemies. That's a surprising thing Jesus said!**

Today we'll explore what Jesus meant and how we can love people who seem so unlovable. We'll talk about how to love everyone—even the meanies!

Surprising Sayings Game

FRENEMIES FLIP

Time: about 10 minutes
Supplies: table, plastic cups (1 per child), stopwatch

Ask each child to place a cup, bottom facing up, on the edge of the table. The cup needs to extend about one inch over the edge of the tabletop. Explain that the goal of this game is to place one finger under the part of the cup extending out and then snap your finger upward so that the cup lifts and flips up onto the table, landing on its bottom.

Each time a child makes a successful flip, he or she will call out "Frenemies Flip!" Say: **See how many times you can get your cup successfully flipped in two minutes. I'll keep track of the time. Ready? Go!**

After two minutes, have kids report how many times they were successful in flipping their cups. Then play again, this time for only one minute. When one minute has passed, applaud the kids' efforts and collect the cups. Ask: **Does anyone know what the word** *frenemy* **means?** Affirm participation to encourage kids to risk giving a "wrong" answer in future sessions.

Say: **Sometimes a person can be a friend one day and an enemy the next day. Everything is fine, and then a friend says or does something hurtful. And when friends hurt us, it** *really* **hurts. We expect friends to be kind and caring at all times.**

Hold your cup so the bottom is facing up and say: **When a friend hurts us, we can shut down and protect ourselves. Nothing can get into this cup right now.** Flip the cup over so the open end is on top. **But if we decide to stay open to people who hurt us—to still care about them and treat** them well—friendships can often heal. And we can decide to forgive people who hurt us. Jesus was an open-cup sort of guy, and he asks us to be the same. Let's hear what Jesus had to say about frenemies and enemies of all kinds.

Surprising Sayings **Bible Story**

GO TO YOUR CORNER

Time: about 15 minutes
Supplies: Bible

Ask a willing child to read Matthew 5:43–47 aloud. Or you can read the passage aloud yourself. After reading the passage, say: **God gives sunshine to good people and bad people. God lets it rain on people who are nice and people who bully others.**

That's what God does. But if you were in charge, what would *you* do? Would you show love to everyone, even awful people who are mean to others? How about people who cheat and steal? Would you give your friends a little extra sunshine and let it rain a little longer on bad people?

> **AGE-ALERT TIPS**
>
> The best way to recruit a willing reader is to do it *before* it's time to read. Ask **older kids** individually if they're willing to read as they come in the door or, after the session, ask if they might be willing to read during other sessions. And don't ignore **younger children** as potential readers—they might surprise you!

If you'd keep things the same—so good and bad people are both loved and treated the same—go to that corner. (point to a corner in the room) **If you'd make some changes, go to that corner.** (point to a different corner)

Once the kids are in their corners (it's okay if they all picked the same corner), say: **Now talk together about why you picked the corner you're in.** Give kids time to talk. Then ask kids in each corner to explain why they made their decision. After the kids share their reasons, discuss:

- **What might happen if God didn't treat everyone in a loving way?**

- If people in the other corner get their way, what might go wrong? What might go right?

After the discussion, say: **I'm glad God is calling the shots, aren't you?** Have kids sit in a circle, then continue: **It's surprising that Jesus says we should love our enemies because that's not how we usually treat enemies. We're not nice to people who aren't nice to us. We don't even like being around them!**

But remember this: *we* used to be God's enemies. Before we decided to follow Jesus, we didn't love or obey God. We ignored him. We didn't thank him for the good things he brought into our lives. We quit being God's enemies and became his friends when we decided to love and follow Jesus.

So let's treat our enemies, the mean people in our lives, as Jesus treats us. Jesus loves everyone. And let's do what Jesus told us to do: let's pray for our enemies. That's one way to love everyone—even the meanies!

CLOSING PRAYER

ENEMY UPLIFT
Time: about 5 minutes
Supplies: none

Say: **Please hold up an index finger.** (pause) **Keep holding up your index finger while we pray. This is a reminder of the bully you have, the same bully you're going to pray for now. Close your eyes and picture that bully in your mind.** (pause)

Sometimes people are bullies because they've been hurt themselves. Ask God to heal any hurts in the life of the bully you have in mind. (pause) Ask God to help the bully feel his love. (pause) **And now ask God to help the bully see his love through how you treat the bully.** (pause) **Amen!**

EXTRA-TIME ACTIVITY-OPTION 1

ONLY GOOD WORDS
Time: about 10 minutes, depending on attendance
Supplies: scraps of paper, pen, container (bowl, box, basket, or paper bag), chair

On each scrap of paper, write a common word such as *yes*, *no*, *my*, *because*, *for*, and *can*. You'll need one word for each child. Put the scraps of paper in a container.

One at a time, have the kids draw a slip of paper from the container and have one child take a seat in the center of the room, the hot seat. The child in the hot seat will read aloud the word on his or her paper—a word that he or she is now forbidden to say again.

Other kids can then ask questions about any topic, and the person in the hot seat must answer in complete sentences. The goal of the rest of the class is to get the person in the hot seat to say the forbidden word on the slip of paper.

The goal of the person in the hot seat is to *not* use the forbidden word. Have kids take turns in the hot seat. See how long those in the hot seat can last before using their forbidden words. To wrap up, say: **One way to love our enemies is to not say mean things about them. But like we just found out, it's tough to control what we say!** Discuss:

- **How can *not* saying mean things about a bully be a way to love that person?**
- **When is it important to tell grown-ups about mean kids? How would you do that?**

EXTRA-TIME ACTIVITY—OPTION 2

NOT ALL BAD

Time: about 10 minutes
Supplies: index cards (or piece of paper, 1 per child), pencils

Ask children to join you sitting in a circle. Say: **When we don't like people, we often quit noticing anything good in them. But even meanies are good in *some* way!**

Let's practice noticing good things in others. On your card, write two good things you can see in the person seated to your right. Maybe the person has a nice smile, is funny, or did something nice for someone today.

It's okay if you don't know the person—you can write two things you like about him or her that you can see right now. Maybe a nice shirt or a perfect nose, for example. You only have two minutes! After two minutes, read aloud what you wrote about the person on your right. Then go around the circle, everyone reading aloud what he or she wrote. When you're all finished, give the cards to the people they're about.

EXTRA-TIME ACTIVITY–OPTION 3

CUPSIDE DOWN
Time: about 5 minutes
Supplies: plastic cups used earlier, plus a few more

Separate the children into groups of four. If you have just a few kids, separate them into pairs. Keeps kids of similar ages together. If you're working with groups of four kids, seat them on the floor with two kids side by side facing the other two kids, who are also sitting side by side. Place about nine plastic cups between the two pairs of kids (use an odd number of cups). Ask the kids to turn about half the cups so the top is facing up and the other half so the bottoms are facing up. Then ask them to decide which pair in their foursome is the "bottoms-up" team and which is the "tops-up" team.

Say: **In your groups, the bottoms-up team will try to turn the cups so they're all bottoms up. The tops-up team will try to turn cups so they're all tops up. There are three rules:**

1. **You can't touch other hands or take cups away from the other pair.**
2. **You can't hold a cup for more than two seconds before turning it.**
3. **When I call time, only the cups are on the floor will count.**

You'll have 20 seconds to get every cup the way you like it. Go!

Play several times, varying the length of each round. Don't go longer than twenty seconds. After each round, have the groups count their cups. After the last round, have kids turn all the cups to the tops-up position. Say: **This week, let's find ways to pour kindness into the lives of everyone, including the meanies!**

Jesus Said ...

Turn the Other Cheek

The Point: Don't try to even up the score.
Scripture Connect: Matthew 5:38–39

Supplies for all session 2 activities options: pennies, string, scissors, markers, rubber bands (size 33 works well), balloons (1 per child), Bible

The Basics for Leaders

There's a reason superheroes are so popular: they show up to even the score. A twisted mastermind plotting to overthrow the world? Enter someone in a spandex suit to right what's wrong. Kids—and adults too—love seeing bad guys get what's coming to them. And we cheer when good guys get revenge for bad stuff done to them.

But Jesus says that's not how things work in his kingdom. He says it's not a good idea to insist that scores be settled or that we get payback. In fact, Jesus says we should not only avoid taking revenge but also *love* those who make our lives difficult. A surprising saying? You bet—and one that you and your kids will explore in this session.

OPENING ACTIVITY–OPTION 1

TELL ME THUMBTHING

Time: about 5 minutes, depending on attendance
Supplies: none

After the kids arrive, say: **When people like a movie, they sometimes give it a thumbs-up.** (demonstrate) **If they really like the movie, they give it two thumbs-up. If they dislike or really dislike the movie, they give it one or two thumbs-down.** (demonstrate)

Say: **Please rate how this past week has gone for you. Was it a one or two thumbs-up week? A one or two thumbs-down week? Or maybe you'd give it one thumbs-up and one thumbs-down—it was a good *and* bad week. Rate your week now.**

After kids rate their weeks, give them 30 seconds each to explain why they rated their weeks as they did. You'll go first, sharing a story that models the sort of brief, personal stories you hope kids will share too.

Children will express themselves more over time, and hearing their stories will help you adapt this session to make it even more relevant to your kids' lives.

OPENING ACTIVITY-OPTION 2

PENNY LIP SHOWDOWN

Time: about 10 minutes
Supplies: pennies (1 per child)

Give each child a penny and ask kids to pair up. If you have an odd number of children, join in yourself. Demonstrate how to hold a penny between your lower lip and chin (scrunch down your lower lip), then ask kids to stand back-to-back with their partners and place their pennies between their lower lips and chins.

Say: **When I say, "Turn the other cheek," quickly turn around and face your partner. The goal is to keep your penny in place longer than your partner can. You can't touch your penny or your partner, but if you make your partner laugh, his or her penny may drop. Ready? Turn the other cheek!**

Play several rounds, adding challenges as you go: standing on one foot, hopping, or saying the alphabet while keeping the penny in place.

Gather up the pennies and say: **When Jesus told his followers to turn the other cheek, he was thinking of something else, something far harder than what we just tried. Let's find out about it after a game.**

Surprising Sayings Game

SURESHOT

Time: about 10 minutes
Supplies: string, scissors, markers, rubber bands (at least 6 per child), inflated balloons (1 per child)

Use string to create a circle on the floor in the middle of the room. If you have 15 or so kids, a circle roughly nine feet across will work. Use less string with fewer kids.

Help each child inflate and tie a balloon. If a child has a latex allergy, let him or her participate at the level that's appropriate—if needed, ask him or her be a referee.

Using markers, ask the kids to write their names on their balloons and then place them in the center of the circle. After all the balloons are in the circle, distribute at least six rubber bands to each child.

Say: **The goal of this game is to shoot your rubber bands from outside the circle to either knock someone else's balloon out of the circle or keep yours inside the circle.**

Tell the kids that the child whose name is written on the last balloon to be knocked outside the circle is the winner. Say: **Once your balloon is knocked out of play, it's done—but you aren't. Use the rest of your rubber bands to get even with whoever shot your balloon out of play by shooting at *his or her* balloon.**

Explain the rules:

1. Shoot only at balloons, not people.
2. When I call "Reload," pick up rubber bands and get ready to shoot again.
3. You can only move a balloon by hitting it with a rubber band, but you can move around the outside of the circle.
4. If a balloon bursts, it's out of play.

Ready? Go! Stop the action to let the kids pick up the rubber bands every 30 to 45 seconds. When the last balloon has been taken out of play, gather up the rubber bands and discuss:

- How did it feel to have someone knock your balloon out of play?
- How much did you want payback—to shoot the balloons of people who shot your balloon?
- Tell about a time when you wanted to get even with someone.

Say: **We don't like people treating us or even our balloons badly. When that happens, we usually want to get even. But Jesus said something surprising: when others are mean to us, we *shouldn't* try to get back at them. Let's hear what Jesus says about that and about turning the other cheek.**

Surprising Sayings Bible Story

JUDGE AND JURY

Time: about 20 minutes
Supplies: Bible

Ask a willing child to read Matthew 5:38–39 aloud. No volunteers? You can read the passage aloud yourself. After reading the passage, say: **Jesus knew the people listening to him thought it was fair to do to others what had been done to them. They thought that because it's in the Old Testament.**

Read Leviticus 24:19–20 aloud. Afterward, say: **Hmm ... it sounds like the Bible says it's okay to settle scores. If a person hurts you, you can hurt that person right back—so long as you don't hurt them more than they hurt you. Seems fair, doesn't it? But let's see how it plays out.**

Tell the kids that you've appointed them as judges. They'll decide what eye-for-an-eye punishment to give three criminals. (Small group? You can always

TIPS

The kingdom of God is built on forgiveness and grace, not revenge. You can tell your kids that, but the truth you share may just roll off them. Let them grapple with that kingdom truth and discover it for themselves. Don't jump in too quickly to give the "right" answer; trust that the Holy Spirit is working in your kids to draw them closer to seeing their world as Jesus sees it.

accuse a kid of more than one crime!) Point to a child and announce that she threw a rock that knocked out the front teeth of another child. Say: **Okay, judges, what punishment should we give this tooth-knocker-outer?**

Lead the judges in discussing what's a fair eye-for-an-eye punishment. Then say: **Before we punish anyone, let's hear about the other two criminals.** Point to another child and say that he stole a candy bar. Unfortunately, he ate it before he was captured. Lead another eye-for-an-eye discussion with the judges until they agree on a punishment.

Then point to a third child and announce that she let a neighbor's dog off a leash so the dog could play. The dog ran away, never to return. Mention that the guilty child doesn't own a pet, so an eye-for-an-eye solution can't be about her dog. Lead a discussion that ends with a punishment for the crime. Say: **Thank you, judges. By the way, I'm pardoning our criminals!** Discuss:

- What made deciding the punishments easy? What made deciding the punishments hard?
- What's something someone could do that would be so bad, there's no eye-for-an-eye solution?

Say: **The eye-for-an-eye way to settle scores doesn't always work. You can't always make everything come out even in the end. Jesus knows that, and he has a fix for the problem: if someone slaps you on one cheek, don't try to settle the score. Instead, turn your head so they can slap the other cheek.** Discuss:

- Do you think Jesus is saying you should let people beat you up? Or is he saying something else? What do you think he means?
- If we're not supposed to keep score, what would Jesus have us do instead?

Say: **Keeping score is a lot of work. And when we're busy keeping score, it's hard to pay attention to Jesus. Instead of always trying to get even with people, I can do what Jesus does: love, forgive, and treat others the way I want to be treated. That's hard, but we don't have to do it alone.**

CLOSING PRAYER

TURNAROUND PRAYER
Time: about 2 minutes
Supplies: none

Say: **Sometimes, even if you forgive someone for hurting you, there are consequences. If I break your nose and you forgive me, you still have a broken nose, and my parents will definitely talk to me about it! No matter what happens to us, we can do what Jesus says and choose to not get even.**

Ask the kids to stand and close their eyes. Then ask them to clench both their fists as hard as they can and picture the face of someone who has been mean to them. Pause for ten seconds before continuing: **Maybe, as you're thinking of that mean person, you want to get even. But instead, you can turn the other cheek. You can give up your right to get an eye for an eye. If you're willing to turn the other cheek, unclench your fists and relax your hands. Now please keep that mean person's face in mind as I pray for us. God, it's hard to turn the other cheek. Please help us by filling us with your love. Amen.**

EXTRA-TIME ACTIVITY—OPTION 1

EVENING UP THE SCORE
Time: about 10 minutes, depending on attendance
Supplies: pennies (1 per child, plus some extras), Bible

Give each child a penny. Have the kids form pairs, sit on the floor, and practice flipping their pennies.

If flipping pennies is hard for kids, they could hold the penny in their cupped hands, shake their hands, and drop the penny to the floor. This works just as well as flipping them.

> **AGE-ALERT TIPS**
> Some **younger children** might not be able to flip coins, so encourage **older kids** to help them.

Say: **Let's see how well you and your partner can even up the score. Each of your coins has a heads and a tails. If you flip your coin 20 times, it seems like the coin should come up heads 10 times and tails 10 times.**

But will it? Tell pairs of kids to help each other keep count as they flip their coins 20 times. Challenge pairs to see how close they get to a 10-heads/10-tails perfect split. Flip coins, report results, and then ask: **What would you like about living in a world where everybody got what they deserved? What wouldn't you like?**

Read Romans 6:23 aloud and then say: **I'm glad I don't get what I deserve! I'm glad God doesn't even up the score with me! Instead, I can accept God's free gift of eternal life through Jesus.**

EXTRA-TIME ACTIVITY—OPTION 2

ADD 'EM UP
Time: about 5 minutes
Supplies: pennies (5 per child)

Have the children form pairs and give each child five pennies. Ask kids to hold the pennies in their left hands and then put both hands behind their backs. Say: **The goal of this game is for you to move some of your coins to your right hand without your partner knowing how many you've moved.**

When I say "Go," move some coins to your right hand. When I say "Stop," put your right hand in front of you and show your partner how many coins you're holding. You win the round if you're holding one more coin than your partner.** Play at least five rounds. Collect coins from kids and discuss:

- **How do you feel when someone has a little more than you? Maybe a better bike, a nicer room, or more money?**
- **Tell about a time when you had a little more than someone else. How did you feel?**

Say: **When someone has more than you or something nicer than you, don't try to even the score. Instead, treat others the way you want to be treated and turn the other cheek.**

EXTRA-TIME ACTIVITY—OPTION 3

DO IT AGAIN?
Time: about 10 minutes
Supplies: none

Ask the kids to sit in a circle. If you have more than six kids, form smaller circles of three or four kids per circle. Say: **In a moment, I'll ask you to consider telling the rest of us about a time when you evened up the score.** (Briefly share an age-appropriate story about a time when you took revenge or tried to get even with someone and how you felt about it then and now.)

Say: **Your turn. Tell us about a time when you got even. How did you feel about it then and how do you feel about it now? After hearing what Jesus wants us to do, answer this question: Would you do it again?**

After kids share, say: **Let's ask for God's help in not wanting to even up the score.** Pray: **God, thank you for not evening up the score with us. Thank you for loving us when we didn't know or love you. Help us love others like you love us. Amen.**

Jesus Said ...

Your Thoughts Matter

The Point: Your thoughts matter, just like your actions.
Scripture Connect: Matthew 5:21–22

Supplies for all session 3 activities options: pillowcase, soft objects to put into the pillowcase (towel, sweater, stuffed animal, yarn), soccer ball, socks, bandannas, Bible, string, scissors, wastebasket, index cards (5 per child)

The Basics for Leaders

We can get in trouble for what we do—that is hardly surprising. Make a huge mistake at work or show up an hour late for dinner at home, and you'll hear about it. But getting in trouble with God because of what you *think*? Not only is that surprising, but it also somehow feels unfair. Yet Jesus drives home a kingdom truth here: God cares more about our hearts than our actions because our hearts drive our actions.

As you help your children explore this surprising saying of Jesus, you'll help them bring Jesus himself into sharper focus. Not as a busybody who spies on their thoughts so he can later punish them but as a friend who knows them—everything about them—and loves them anyway.

And kids will discover that they play a leading role when it comes to their thoughts: they can choose to focus on what helps them love and follow Jesus.

OPENING ACTIVITY-OPTION 1

TELL ME THUMBTHING

Time: about 5 minutes, depending on attendance
Supplies: none

After the kids arrive, say: **When people like a movie, they sometimes give it a thumbs-up.** (demonstrate) **If they really like the movie, they give it two thumbs-up. If they dislike or really dislike the movie, they give it one or two thumbs-down.** (demonstrate)

Say: **Please rate how this past week has gone for you. Was it a one or two thumbs-up week? A one or two thumbs-down week? Or maybe you'd give it one thumbs-up and one thumbs-down—it was a good *and* bad week. Rate your week now.**

After kids rate their weeks, give them 30 seconds each to explain why they rated their weeks as they did. You'll go first, sharing a story that models the sort of brief, personal stories you hope kids will share too.

Children will express themselves more over time, and hearing their stories will help you adapt this session to make it even more relevant to your kids' lives.

OPENING ACTIVITY-OPTION 2

WHAT DO YOU THINK?

Time: about 10 minutes
Supplies: pillowcase, soft items to put into the pillowcase (towel, sweater, stuffed animal, yarn), soccer ball

Before the kids arrive, tuck a soft object into the pillowcase and tie it shut. Keep the other items hidden. Tell kids to pass around the pillowcase. They'll each have seven seconds to *silently* feel what's inside and think about what it could be. After everyone has had a turn, ask kids to call out—at the same time—what they think is inside.

TIP

Do you have more than 12 kids? Use two pillowcases with identical items inside. Or form children into pairs and give each pair seven seconds to inspect the pillowcase and then decide together what's inside.

Then reveal what's really in the pillowcase. Play several rounds with different items. For the last round, put the soccer ball inside the pillowcase and give kids four seconds to feel it. When finished, say: **You thought about what was inside. Then you acted on your thought by calling out your guess.**

Our thoughts are important because they guide our actions. If we're *thinking* the right things, it's a lot easier to *do* the right things. Jesus had some surprising things to say about how much our thoughts matter. We'll find out what he said, but first, let's play a game!

Surprising Sayings Game

PIRATE SOCK TOSS

Time: about 10 minutes
Supplies: socks, bandannas

Have the kids form pairs. Give each pair a clean, rolled-up sock. One child in each pair should stand against a wall, facing the center of the room. Then about 10 paces away, have the second child in each pair face his or her partner.

Say: **The game of Pirate Sock Toss might have once been played by pirates while sailing the high seas! Let's practice our pirate words, starting with "Aaargh!"** Lead children in practicing a pirate "Aaargh!" Then have them practice "Walk the plank!" and "Polly wants a cracker!" Now say: **Please scrunch one eye closed as if you're wearing an eye patch. Keep that eye closed until I tell you to open both eyes.**

> ### AGE-ALERT TIPS
> **Younger children** may struggle with keeping one eye closed without closing both eyes. Have bandannas on hand so you can tie them around children's heads to cover one eye. **Older kids** who struggle can simply hold one hand over an eye.

Ask pairs to take turns tossing a sock to one another. While tossing, they're to growl, "Aaargh!" When children catch a sock, they're to say, "Polly wants a cracker!" When they drop a sock, they're to call out, "Walk the plank!"

Gradually move kids closer together. Once they've thrown and caught from three paces apart, have them go back to 10 paces and try tossing and catching with both eyes open. Collect socks and have everyone sit together.

Say: **Was it easier to catch a sock with one eye open or with both eyes open?** (pause) **When you have two eyes open, each of your eyes sees the sock from a slightly different angle. That helps your brain figure out how close the sock is, which helps you catch it. Depth perception is something you don't notice until you close one eye and lose it. That's why we pirate sock catchers need to think clearly about where socks are so we can snag them.**

When we think clearly, we can act accordingly. Our thoughts matter, just like our actions! In Jesus's day, some people weren't thinking clearly. They thought that as long as they didn't kill and curse, God would think they were okay. But Jesus said that God doesn't just care about our actions—he cares about our thoughts too!

Surprising Sayings Bible Story

"THINK-ABOUT-IT" TWO-STEP
Time: about 20 minutes
Supplies: Bible

Ask a willing child to read Matthew 5:21–22 aloud. No volunteers? You can read the passage aloud yourself.

Have the kids stand together in the middle of the room. Tell them that depending on how they answer a question, they'll take two steps in whatever direction you send them. For instance, if they prefer soda, have them take two steps to the left. If they prefer lemonade, have them take two steps to the right. Use the following choices and directions to move the kids around:

TIP
If you identified a child at your last session who was willing to read, ask that child to do the honors. Before the kids leave, see if you can rustle up a few more to serve as readers in the future.

- donut or bagel: two steps forward or backward
- soccer or swimming: two steps left or right
- save money or spend money: two steps forward or backward
- pizza or tacos: two steps left or right
- math or science: two steps left or right

- gym class or English class: two steps forward or backward
- read a book or watch a movie: two steps left or right
- beach or mountains: two steps forward or backward
- play music or listen to music: two steps left or right
- ride a bike or ride a horse: two steps forward or backward

Ask kids to notice how far apart they've gotten. Then have everyone sit down. Say: **You just thought about and made 10 decisions. Each decision brought you closer to someone or farther away. That's also true with God. Our thoughts and decisions can draw us closer to God or lead us further away from him. Our thoughts matter because they determine what we do.** Discuss:

- **Tell us about something you decided to do that drew you closer to God.**
- **Share something that led you farther away from God.**

Say: **Jesus says that anger and name calling are a sign of what's going on in our hearts—of what we're thinking and feeling. Our thoughts matter, just like our actions.**

CLOSING PRAYER

ANYWHERE HIDE AND SEEK
Time: about 5 minutes
Supplies: none

Say: **Your thoughts and imagination can take you anywhere. For instance, imagine we're playing hide and seek and you're one-inch tall. Look around the room and pick the spot you'd hide. Don't tell anyone where it is.**

Have kids form pairs. Say: **You can ask your partner up to five yes or no questions before guessing the partner's hiding spot. For this to work, we've all got to be honest.** Allow time for partners to play.

Say: **That's the power of your thoughts. You can imagine yourself an inch tall, hiding in someone's shirt pocket. Our thoughts let us invent new things, create fantastic movies, and solve all kinds of problems. But they can also lead us to tell lies, do wrong things, and hurt others.**

Let's ask God to be the Lord of our thoughts and actions. Ask kids to close their eyes. Pray: **God, thank you for loving us and wanting to know us better. We're glad that you want us to know you too. God, what would you have us do this week? Use our thoughts to help us think of something to do that would please you.** (pause as children pray silently) **Thank you, God, for the thoughts you give us. We want to use our thoughts for you. Amen.**

EXTRA-TIME ACTIVITY—OPTION 1

NINJA CARDS

Time: about 10 minutes, depending on attendance
Supplies: Bible, string, scissors, wastebasket, small index cards (5 per child)

Say: **We can't control what we think, right? Actually ... we can. And we're going to get some practice.**

Read Philippians 4:8 aloud, then say: **We *can* decide what to think about. We can think about things that help us know, love, and follow Jesus. And we can decide to *not* think about things that get in the way of our friendship with Jesus.** Ask: **What's something you could think about that's true, honorable, right, and pure?**

Say: **Let's see what else might be good to think about as we play a game of Ninja Cards.**

Using string, create a circle on the floor around the wastebasket. Leave four feet between the basket and the string. Give each child five index cards. Explain that the goal of the game is to toss all the cards into the basket. Tell the kids the rules:

1. The cards can't be folded or crumpled up.
2. The cards must be released without your hands crossing the line—no leaning!
3. When releasing a card, you must call out something that's true, honorable, right, or pure.

Play as long as kids can think of things to call out. Repeat those items kids say that you can endorse.

EXTRA-TIME ACTIVITY-OPTION 2

AUTOPILOT NOSE

Time: about 5 minutes
Supplies: none

Say: **Sometimes what we think is true isn't true. For instance, you might think you can fly. As you jump off the roof, you might be sure you can fly, but your newly broken leg says otherwise.**

Cross the middle and index fingers on your right hand. (demonstrate) **Now close your eyes. Once your eyes are closed, place the tips of both those crossed fingers on the tip of your nose so each finger is on one side of your nose. It feels as if you have two noses, doesn't it?** Ask kids to open their eyes.

Say: **You just fooled your brain because it's not used to getting information from your fingers when they're crossed. And because your brain tries to make sense of everything, it's not sure what to do. Your eyes are closed, so your brain can't see what's going on.** Discuss:

- **What can this experiment tell us about always trusting our thoughts?**
- **Where do you go for advice when things don't make sense to you?**

Say: **As for me, I like to check in with God when things don't make sense. I can pray and talk things over with God, read what the Bible says, and talk with friends who also follow Jesus. Our thoughts matter, just like our actions.**

EXTRA-TIME ACTIVITY-OPTION 3

AND THE QUESTION IS ...

Time: about 10 minutes
Supplies: none

Say: **I'm going to read an answer. Your job is to figure out a question that fits it. And you can't use a phone!** Share this example: **Millard Fillmore is** the answer. **A correct question would be some version of "Who is the thirteenth president of the United States?"** You can decide how much detail is required for a question to be correct.

Form two teams (a team can be just one child if you have a small group). After giving an answer, give teams 20 seconds to brainstorm a question. Alternate which team goes first in offering an answer and award points. Five points: they *nailed* it. Two points: they convince you that their question works. One point: they're completely wrong, but nice try! Here are some answers with questions:

- **105 pounds of skin:** How much skin flakes off an average person in a lifetime?
- **The Tanzanian parasitic wasp:** What's the world's smallest winged insect?
- **18 to 22 hours per day:** How much do koalas sleep?
- **At least 10,000 times better than you can do it:** How well does my dog smell stuff?
- **The African bush elephant, which can weigh 11 tons:** What's the largest land animal?
- **A mare:** What do you call a female horse?
- **Gopher wood:** What wood was used to build Noah's ark?
- **You do it more than 20,000 times per day—and probably don't notice:** How often do I blink?

Say: **Some things you either know or don't know; no amount of thinking helps you suddenly know about wasps. But the really important stuff in life—who to follow, who to love, how to live your life—takes some thought. And it takes getting some advice too.**

Let's invite God to give us advice when we're thinking about the big stuff. Pray: **God, thank you for loving us. Thank you for knowing us and what's best for us. Please guide our thoughts and our actions. Amen.**

Jesus Said ...

Don't Worry

The Point: Don't worry—trust God.
Scripture Connect: Matthew 6:25–27

Supplies for all session 4 activities options: 2 rolls of toilet paper, paper (1 sheet per child), Bible, pencil, balloon, pin, pencil, plastic spoons (1 per child), 1 jar of baby food, stopwatch

The Basics for Leaders

Adults aren't the only ones who worry—kids do too. And in their world, there's plenty to worry about: homework assignments that pile up daily, relationships, the future, what will happen if their parents divorce. For some kids, life can be one anxious moment after another.

In Jesus's day, there was plenty to worry about too. Living in an occupied country made life uncertain. At any moment, Roman soldiers could sweep through and take whatever they wanted, killing anyone who stood in their way.

Yet Jesus said to not worry because there's someone who can be trusted to provide and protect. You're going to help children discover that because God's in control, we don't have to worry or be afraid.

OPENING ACTIVITY–OPTION 1

TELL ME THUMBTHING
Time: about 5 minutes, depending on attendance
Supplies: none

After the kids arrive, say: **When people like a movie, they sometimes give it a thumbs-up.** (demonstrate) **If they really like the movie, they give it two thumbs-up. If they dislike or really dislike the movie, they give it one or two thumbs-down.** (demonstrate)

Say: **Please rate how this past week has gone for you. Was it a one or two thumbs-up week? A one or two thumbs-down week? Or maybe you'd give it one thumbs-up and one thumbs-down—it was a good** *and* **bad week. Rate your week now.**

After kids rate their weeks, give them 30 seconds each to explain why they rated their weeks as they did. You'll go first, sharing a story that models the sort of brief, personal stories you hope kids will share too.

Children will express themselves more over time, and hearing their stories will help you adapt this session to make it even more relevant to your kids' lives.

OPENING ACTIVITY–OPTION 2

ALL THAT YOU NEED

Time: about 10 minutes
Supplies: roll of toilet paper

Ask the kids to sit in a circle. Tell them that they'll be passing around a roll of toilet paper and should take as many squares as they need. You can begin by taking three squares. Don't answer when kids ask, "Need for *what*?"

Once the roll has reached you again, say: **For each square you took, I'd like you to tell us one thing about yourself that most of us wouldn't know. Maybe it's a favorite food or where you were born.**

Go first and share three facts about your life, then encourage kids to do the same as you go around the circle. If a child took 30 squares, ask for just a few facts so the activity moves along. After all kids have shared, ask: **If you'd known what I was going to ask you to do, would you have changed how many squares you took?**

Say: **Sometimes when I'm making a decision, I wish I had more information. I worry that I'll make a mistake or that things won't work out. Today we're talking about worry. Jesus surprised people with what he had to say about worry. Let's see if we're surprised too.**

Surprising Sayings Game

PRESSURE'S ON

Time: about 10 minutes
Supplies: paper (1 sheet per child), roll of toilet paper

Give each child a sheet of paper. Ask the kids to stand and spread out so there's an arm's length between them. Have kids crumple their sheets of paper into a ball. Place the roll of toilet paper on a chair so the inside tube is aiming toward the children.

Say: **It may not look like it, but the tube in this roll of toilet paper is a camera. Scouts from your favorite sports teams are watching. They've heard how fast and talented you are, and this is your tryout to be a professional athlete. This is a once-in-a-lifetime opportunity, but ... no pressure. It's do or die, but no pressure.**

Ask the kids to toss their paper balls in the air and catch them. Say: **That's the first test. So far, you're all doing great. But there are more tests!** Add these challenges, one at a time, as kids toss their paper balls and catch them:

- spin in a circle before catching it
- clap five times before catching it
- spin in a circle and clap twice before catching it
- touch your knees before catching it
- catch it behind your back
- catch it with only your left hand

Have the kids sit down. Pick up the roll of toilet paper and examine it. Say: **Oops—looks like I grabbed the wrong roll. This is just a cardboard tube after all. Oh, well.** Discuss:

- **How did it feel to know that if you messed up, you'd lose out on a future of fame and fortune?**
- **When do you feel under pressure to perform?**
- **What are some situations in which you worry you won't do well enough?**

Allow the children to answer. As they share, you're finding out how you can pray for them. Say: **Jesus talked about worry and what to do with it. Let's hear what he had to say.**

Surprising Sayings Bible Story

REWIND

Time: about 20 minutes
Supplies: Bible, crumpled paper balls from the game, pencil, paper

Ask a willing child to read Matthew 5:25–27 aloud. No volunteers? You can read the passage aloud yourself. Help the children get into pairs. Using their two crumpled paper balls, pairs will build a bird's nest. They can rip the paper into strips, flatten it out, and shape it however they wish, but they have to somehow add to their nest with every idea that comes up in response to a question you'll ask.

Say: **In the passage we just read, Jesus said birds don't grow their own food, but God still takes care of them. My question is this: In what other ways does God take care of birds? With each way we can think of, you and your partner need to somehow add to the nest you're building. If we come up with enough ideas about how God cares for birds, you'll have a nest any bird would be proud to call home!**

As kids brainstorm ideas, jot them down. Repeat the ideas one at a time, allowing 20 to 30 seconds for pairs to somehow modify their nests. Some possible answers include God provides water, flight, warm feathers, flocks of friends, great eyesight (eagles), and the ability to soar for hours (hawks).

When the nests are complete, allow pairs to examine one another's creations. Applaud all efforts. Say: **Now let's consider our own nests—our lives. In what ways does God take care of us?**

Allow the kids to share responses. Dig deep. Ask about how God cares for us physically, emotionally, and spiritually. Say: **When Jesus said what he said, those listening to him were probably surprised. Don't worry? They had *plenty* to worry about! Like the birds, many people didn't know where they'd get enough food to eat. They lived in a time and place where medical help was poor. They lived in a country that had been invaded by Rome, so enemy soldiers were everywhere.**

Of course these people were worried—they had good reason! So just telling them not to worry wouldn't work. Instead, Jesus told them to trust God.

Read Matthew 6:26 aloud and then say: **Nothing against our feathered friends, but Jesus is saying you're far more important than birds. God has created you for a friendship with him that only you can have, and part of that friendship is trust. Trust that God knows and loves you. Trust that God wants what's best for you. Don't worry—trust God!**

CLOSING PRAYER

BALLOON POP PRAYER
Time: about 5 minutes
Supplies: balloon, pin

With the children watching, inflate a balloon and tie it off. Hold up the balloon and a pin. Say: **Jesus never said that because we trust God, bad things won't happen. People who love Jesus still get sick. They still flunk tests. Others are still sometimes mean to them. But when bad things happen, people who love Jesus have someone to help them—Jesus! He walks with us through all the tough stuff.**

Ask the kids to close their eyes. Keep moving around the room as you speak so you increase the children's anticipation as they await a loud *pop*.

Say: **I've got a balloon and a pin. At some point, I'll pop this balloon. When I do, there will be a loud, earsplitting noise. I might be holding the balloon far from you or right next to your ear. There's no way for you to know because your eyes are closed and I'm like a ninja—stealthy and quiet.** (pause) **Is the bang coming now ... or later? You don't know.**

Pop the balloon over *your* head so it's not near any child's ears. Then say: **Whew! The tension was getting to me! Maybe you were worried I'd pop the balloon right next to you. Or maybe you were worried I *wouldn't* do that.**

We worry about what might happen in the future or what happened in the past, but there's nothing we can do about either of those times. The good news for us who love Jesus is that he was with us in the past and he will be with us in the future.

Let's take a few minutes to tell Jesus what worries us about the past. Please close your eyes and put your hands behind your backs. Silently tell Jesus what worries you have from the past. (pause) Now please put your hands in front of you and tell Jesus what worries you have about the future. (pause)

Pray: **Thank you for hearing us, Jesus, and for caring about those things that worry us. Help us trust you with everything, even our worries. Amen.**

EXTRA-TIME ACTIVITY–OPTION 1

BEST LAID PLANS

Time: about 10 minutes, depending on attendance
Supplies: none

Say: **Sometimes, no matter how well we plan, things go wrong. I'll describe a couple things people did, and you tell me all the ways you could imagine things going wrong.**

Share these three scenarios and encourage the kids to imagine all the disasters they can think of that might happen to the people involved:

- **Mason and Jayden decide to go camping on a beach. They set up a tent.**
- **Sophia was positive she could jump the curb on her skateboard.**
- **Calvin saw a dog and decided to pet it.**

After kids exhaust their disaster stories, ask them to discuss the following:

- **Share a time when one of your plans went off track. What happened?**
- **When things go wrong, how easy or hard is it for you to trust God? Why?**
- **What might help you trust God more?**

Say: **When things go wrong, it can be hard to remember that God is in control and we don't have to worry or be afraid. Those are the perfect times to count on God to give us what we need!**

EXTRA-TIME ACTIVITY—OPTION 2

BIRD FOOD

Time: about 5 minutes
Supplies: plastic spoons (1 per child), jar of baby food, stopwatch

Think of this game as a pureed version of Hot Potato. Ask the kids to sit in a circle and give each child a spoon. Hold up the jar of baby food and say: **We'll pass this around the circle until time's up. If you're holding the jar at the end of the time, you'll use your spoon to take a taste. No double-dipping allowed!**

Jesus said that birds don't do anything to grow their food and they still get to eat. You're getting to do the same with this lovely jar of (read the label aloud)**. If the jar is in the process of being passed when time's up, the rest of us will decide who takes a taste.**

Play rounds of varying times, but keep each fairly short. At least once, call time after just two seconds. Be sure the lid is *firmly* secured before starting another round. Play several rounds and then collect the spoons and the baby food. Allow children who need to get some water to do so.

Say: **Jesus cares about us and gives us what we need, including food. Don't worry—trust God!**

EXTRA-TIME ACTIVITY—OPTION 3

GOT YOUR BACK

Time: about 10 minutes
Supplies: none

Have the kids get into pairs. Be careful to form pairs of like-sized children. Have each pair sit back-to-back on the floor, linking their elbows behind them and bending their knees in front of them.

Say, **When I give you the word, lean back on your partner and try to stand up. Trust me, your partner's got your back!** Give the word. Be aware that this takes effort and some pairs may not succeed. If some pairs are unsuccessful, let them trade partners and try again.

Say: **When someone's got your back—is there for you when you're struggling—that's a great thing. When Jesus said that we're valuable to God, he was saying that God's got our back, and there's nobody I trust more to help me when I need help! So don't worry, trust God!**

Jesus Said ...

Be Happy When Others Are Mean to You

The Point: Be joyful—no matter what.
Scripture Connect: Matthew 5:10–12

Supplies for all session 5 activities options: paperback books (1 per child), Bible, masking tape (or painters' tape)

The Basics for Leaders

Here's something nobody expected Jesus to say: when others treat you badly, be happy about it. *What*? Actually, that's not *quite* what He said. Jesus said that if we're living in a way that shows we're following Him and others treat us badly because of it, it's something worth celebrating.

It means that others are seeing Him in us. They're brushing up against the kingdom, feeling the conviction of the followers, and finding that uncomfortable. And it means that they're seeing an on-ramp to life as a follower of Jesus and having to decide whether they want to take it.

In this session, you'll help the children explore what it means to suffer for Jesus and have unshakable joy no matter what happens to them.

OPENING ACTIVITY—OPTION 1

TELL ME THUMBTHING

Time: about 5 minutes, depending on attendance
Supplies: none

After the kids arrive, say: **When people like a movie, they sometimes give it a thumbs-up.** (demonstrate) **If they really like the movie, they give it two thumbs-up. If they dislike or really dislike the movie, they give it one or two thumbs-down.** (demonstrate)

Say: **Please rate how this past week has gone for you. Was it a one or two thumbs-up week? A one or two thumbs-down week? Or maybe you'd give it one thumbs-up and one thumbs-down—it was a good *and* bad week. Rate your week now.**

After kids rate their weeks, give them 30 seconds each to explain why they rated their weeks as they did. You'll go first, sharing a story that models the sort of brief, personal stories you hope kids will share too.

Children will express themselves more over time, and hearing their stories will help you adapt this session to make it even more relevant to your kids' lives.

OPENING ACTIVITY—OPTION 2

HONEY, IF YOU LOVE ME, YOU'LL SMILE

Time: about 10 minutes
Supplies: none

Help the children form pairs, keeping similar-age kids together. Explain that they'll play a game and that the goal of the game is for one person in each pair to make the other smile by saying, "Honey, if you love me, you'll smile." The partner will answer, "Honey Bunny, I love you, but I just can't smile." No tickling or touching of any sort is allowed, but goofy looks and silly voices are okay.

Lead kids in practicing both lines, then ask the person in each pair wearing the most blue to begin. Say: **Try to get your partner to smile. Watch carefully for a reaction—even the trace of a smile counts as a victory. Ready? Go!** After a short time, have partners exchange roles.

Say: **How you delivered your lines was funny—but did you notice what you actually said? One person asked for a smile and the second person said he or she couldn't smile, and that's no fun.**

Jesus said something surprising about how we might respond when we find it hard to smile because people are mean to us. We'll hear what he said, but first, let's play a quick game!

Surprising Sayings Game

UNSHAKABLE STROLL

Time: about 10 minutes
Supplies: paperback books (1 per child)

Give each child a book that you won't mind getting back damaged if it falls on the floor—it will happen! Explain that children were once taught proper posture by placing books on their heads so they could learn to walk without the book falling off. Have kids line up against a wall. Explain the rules for the game:

1. It's not a race—the goal is to get there without the book falling.
2. You can't touch the book to balance it.
3. If a book falls, it's okay to stop and place it on your head again and then continue on from that spot.

Place a book on each kid's head. Say: **Will your books stay steady or slide off? Take an "unshakable stroll" to the other wall. Go!** After kids complete the task, say: **For this next walk, we have the same rules, but this time, it *is* a race. Ready? Set? Stroll!** When they're finished, gather books and ask the kids to sit down. Say: **It seems your books weren't unshakable after all. I'm curious, what in your life is unshakable? What or who can you always depend on?**

Before you answer, let me tell you that in my life ... (Briefly share an age-appropriate response. Pick something or someone that *isn't* God or Jesus. Why? If you go there first, so will all your kids because you've signaled it's the "right" answer.)

Allow time for kids to share, then say: **Books aren't the only shaky things in life. So is our happiness. Our happiness depends on what's happening in our lives. If people are nice to us, we're happy. But if someone's mean, our happiness can disappear, and we become angry or sad.**

Jesus told his followers they could have unshakable happiness that held up even if people were mean to them. In fact, he said they *should* feel happy when people are mean to them—at least sometimes. That's a surprising thing to say. Let's find out what Jesus meant.

Surprising Sayings Bible Story

JOYFUL LIKE JESUS

Time: about 20 minutes
Supplies: Bible

Ask a willing child to read Matthew 5:10–12 aloud. No volunteers? You can read the passage aloud yourself.

Say: **Jesus warned his followers what would happen if they followed him: people would make fun of them, be mean to them, and lie about them. If people make fun of us because we follow Jesus, he says we can be happy about it. That's because we'll know we're living in a way that pleases God, and God**

TIP

If you identified a child at your last session who was willing to read, ask that child to do the honors. Before the kids leave, see if you can rustle up few more to serve as readers in the future.

will reward us. Jesus is *not* saying to be happy when people are mean because we were mean to them first! That *wouldn't* be pleasing to God, and we'd just be getting what we deserve.

Happiness depends on what's going on in your life. If everything's going well, you're happy. But joy is deeper. Joy is happiness you feel even when things are hard, even when people are mean to you.

Ask kids to stand in a single-file line, facing you. Explain that you'll tell them about something that might happen to them, and if that thing would make them happy, they're to take a step to their right. If it would make them unhappy, they're to take a step to the left. Then, when you tell them to, they'll return to their original positions.

Say: **Let's say you missed lunch—your favorite lunch—and now you're really, really hungry.** (pause as kids step to the left or right) **But that's because it was the only time you could pick up free tickets to Disney**

World. Wow, that makes missing lunch a happy thing, huh? Anyone want to change where they're standing?

Allow the kids to shift positions. After they return to the single-file line, have them respond to the following situations. Always give the kids an opportunity to shift spots.

- You got in trouble for being late to school ... because you stopped to rescue a puppy from traffic.
- You were handed a long list of extra chores ... so you could make money to go on a mission trip where you'll help others.
- Your parents had a fight ... but then they made up, and their marriage is better than ever.
- A friend called you a dummy ... because you believe in Jesus.

Thank kids for taking part, and then say: **Let's talk about that last one.**

- Why might people be mean to someone for believing in and following Jesus?
- How have you seen Jesus followers made fun of, lied about, or treated badly? Or have you never seen that?

Say: **In some parts of the world, it's dangerous to follow Jesus. People will hurt Christians—even kill them. But Jesus tells those followers what he tells us: be happy when others are mean to you because of me. Be joyful—no matter what.**

Sometimes I let problems in my life get in the way of my joy. We need help being joyful, so let's ask Jesus for help now.

CLOSING PRAYER

"HELP ME" PRAYER
Time: about 5 minutes
Supplies: none

Ask the kids to find a partner and sit or stand together. Say: **Tell your partner about a time when you found it hard to be joyful.** Allow partners a brief amount of time to talk.

Say: **Now let's pray for our partners. Let's ask Jesus to help our partner feel joy even when people are mean or life is hard. Ask Jesus to help your partner be joyful—no matter what.** (pause while children pray) **God, thank you for joy. Thank you for the joy we can have in our lives. Help our partners feel joy even if people are mean to them. Amen.**

EXTRA-TIME ACTIVITY-OPTION 1

LEAP FOR JOY

Time: about 10 minutes
Supplies: masking tape (or painters' tape)

Using tape, create a line on the floor that's long enough for your kids to stand on while they're lined up side by side. Then every foot, make additional tape lines. Create eight lines at one-foot intervals and then one line at 20 feet, just in case any of your kids is a superhero in disguise.

Say: **Sometimes when someone is joyful, she says that she's so happy, she could "leap for joy." Let's give that a try!** Have the kids line up side by side behind the line, facing the additional ones on the floor. Before they go for a long jump, ask them to stand on the line that reflects how much joy they feel in life right now. If they're just a little joyful, they'll stand on the one-foot line. Really joyful? That might be the six-foot line. Super joyful? They'll be out at the 20-foot line.

After the kids choose a spot to stand, let them explain why they picked that spot. Then say, **Okay, line up next to one another on the starting line and let's see how far you can fly!** If kids are wearing slippery leather-soled shoes or sandals, have them take them off; otherwise, they're ready to go.

Give kids two jumps. Tell them that the goal isn't to beat anyone else but to see if they can jump farther the second time. Afterward, say: **We can have a joyful life even when things aren't going smoothly for us. We can even be happy when others are mean to us because our joy doesn't depend on anything besides our friendship with Jesus!**

EXTRA-TIME ACTIVITY-OPTION 2

OPPOSITES

Time: about 5 minutes
Supplies: none

Say: **When I call out a word, call out the opposite word. Let's see if we all come up with the same opposites.** Use the following list for some examples of words and their opposites. Feel free to add your own:

- deep/shallow
- dawn/dusk
- innie/outtie
- calm/excited
- first/last
- humid/arid
- hard/easy
- higher/lower
- foreigner/native
- freezing/melting
- everybody/nobody

If there's time, invite kids to call out their own words and keep the game going.

Say: **Being happy seems like the opposite of what you'd feel if people were mean to you. But when following Jesus causes problems, those are good problems to have. Jesus said we should be happy when people are mean to us for his sake. Why? Because we'll be rewarded in heaven and because it's a sign that we're doing the right things. We can have an unshakable happiness in Jesus. We can be joyful—no matter what!**

EXTRA-TIME ACTIVITY-OPTION 3

HIGH-WIRE TRYOUTS

Time: about 10 minutes
Supplies: masking tape (or painters' tape)

Use tape to create a line on the floor that's 15 feet long. Tell the children that at one time, when a circus came to town, acrobats walked across a wire strung high in the air. They were unshakable! Announce to kids that they will be trying out for the new high-wire act. Ask kids who aren't on the wire to "ooooh" and "aaaah" in the audience.

Explain the rules:

1. You must stay on the high wire or you'll fall to your doom.
2. You can do anything you think will amaze the audience. You can walk heel-to-toe or on your tiptoes, walk backward, hop, or even dare to walk with your eyes closed.

Who's up for a walk on the high wire?

Let volunteers go first and then encourage other kids to give it a shot. Then say: **You've got to be unshakable on the high wire or you'll fall and land on the clown car or in a tiger cage.**

In life, there are a lot of things that can make us feel like we're shaking—being sick, moving to a new town, having others make fun of us. But we can have an unshakable happiness in Jesus. We can be joyful—no matter what!

Jesus Said ...

I Am the Way, the Truth, and the Life

The Point: Jesus is the only way to God.
Scripture Connect: John 14:6–9

Supplies for all session 6 activities options: 2 keys, string, scissors, red marker, masking tape, Bible, paper, markers, pen

The Basics for Leaders

If anything Jesus said raises eyebrows today, it's this: he claimed to be the way, the truth, and the life—the *only* way to God. In a world where it's expected that every religious belief has equal merit, this is a tough quote to hear. It leaves Jesus sounding exclusive and demanding.

But that's not the case. He's being *inclusive*—offering himself as a bridge to God to all who will accept his sacrifice and forgiveness. Still, he's saying something that's hard to hear. He's saying that knowing him isn't just one of many options but the *only* option. It's possible to learn a great deal about God elsewhere. But to know God? That's knowing Jesus.

In this session, you'll help your children discover this truth: when you meet Jesus, you meet God. Jesus is the only way to God.

OPENING ACTIVITY—OPTION 1

TELL ME THUMBTHING
Time: about 5 minutes, depending on attendance
Supplies: none

After the kids arrive, say: **When people like a movie, they sometimes give it a thumbs-up.** (demonstrate) **If they really like the movie, they give it two thumbs-up. If they dislike or really dislike the movie, they give it one or two thumbs-down.** (demonstrate)

Say: **Please rate how this past week has gone for you. Was it a one or two thumbs-up week? A one or two thumbs-down week? Or maybe you'd give it one thumbs-up and one thumbs-down—it was a good *and* bad week. Rate your week now.**

After kids rate their weeks, give them 30 seconds each to explain why they rated their weeks as they did. You'll go first, sharing a story that models the sort of brief, personal stories you hope kids will share too.

Children will express themselves more over time, and hearing their stories will help you adapt this session to make it even more relevant to your kids' lives.

OPENING ACTIVITY–OPTION 2

"JUST ONE WAY" KEY PASS

Time: about 10 minutes
Supplies: 2 keys, string, scissors, red marker

For this activity, you'll use string, the length of which depends on how many kids you have. For each child, allow six feet of string. However long your string, use a red marker to indicate the middle.

Ask the children to line up in a row. Beginning with a child at one end of the line, have the children each weave about six feet of the string through their arms and legs, through a belt loop, and around their waists.

When the last child in line has gotten wrapped up, give the child on each end a key and these instructions: **At my signal, slide your key onto the string and work it along until it makes its way to the next person in line. You cannot break the string! Your goal is to get the key on your end of the string to the red halfway mark before the key at the other end reaches the mark. And it's okay to get help from someone standing next to you move the key along. Ready? Go!**

Cheer on the kids as they struggle to move their keys along. When one key has reached the red mark, applaud the efforts and have the kids carefully untangle themselves and sit down. Ask: **What made this easy? What made this hard?**

Say: **One thing that made this hard was that there was just one way to get your key to the finish line. Jesus said something surprising about only one way: he said that there's only one way to God. Today we'll dive into what he meant. But first, it's time to risk life and limb on a Laser Danger Course!**

Surprising Sayings Game

LASER DANGER COURSE

Time: about 15 minutes
Supplies: string, scissors, masking tape

For this activity, you'll need a hallway and about ten minutes to prepare. If possible, set up the course where kids won't see it. If you have no time to prep, see the "Punt!" idea.

Using lengths of string and masking tape (that won't remove paint!), create a wall-to-wall maze of strings—some high, some low—up and down a hallway. Be sure that a child will be able to crawl over, through, or under the strings without touching them.

> ### PUNT!
> If there's no time to prep, loop the string around on the floor and group kids into pairs. One child will close his or her eyes, and his or her sighted partner will tell him or her where to step to avoid landing on the string. You can use the same debrief questions.

Gather the kids at one end of the hallway and tell them the strings are fiery lasers that will vaporize anyone who touches them and also set off an alarm. The lasers are protecting a priceless treasure at the other end—one that can be reached only by going through the string.

Say: **Move carefully down the hall without touching a laser.** Cheer the kids on as they go through the maze. When they're at the other end, say: **Guess there's no fiery lasers after all. Or alarm. Or treasure. Everyone run back and don't worry about the lasers!** Ask the kids to find partners and sit down. Say: **Jesus said something surprising. He said *he* was the way, the truth, and the life and the only way to God. Just like there was only one way to the pretend treasure in our game, there's only one way to God. But with Jesus, there really *is* a priceless treasure: a friendship with God!**

I'm excited about being God's friend, so I want to know more about Jesus and everything he said. Let's dive into what Jesus said about being the way, the truth, and the life—and that he's the only way to God!

Surprising Sayings **Bible Story**

ALL ROADS

Time: about 15 minutes
Supplies: Bible, sheet of paper, masking tape

Ask a willing child to read John 14:6–9 aloud. Then have children line up, side by side, facing you. Let them see you tape a piece of paper to the wall behind you.

Say: **When some people hear Jesus saying that he's the only way to God, they get upset. They think there should be lots of ways to God or that one way is as good as another. Let's do an experiment.**

Ask the kids to stand up and close their eyes. Explain that you'll be asking them to take steps in different directions—with their eyes closed. Tell them to do so carefully, because sooner or later, they'll bump into something or someone.

Say: **The piece of paper I hung on the wall represents God. Let's say that to reach God, you've got to be and do** *all* **the right things,** *all* **the time. I'll give you some instructions, and we'll find out how well that works for us. If you have dark hair, take two steps to the right. If you have light hair, take three steps to the left.**

Pause to let kids bump their way to taking steps, then continue. Assign the number of steps you think works best in your space. Here are prompts for taking steps:

- brown eyes / blue eyes / other color eyes
- like math / don't like math
- pray every day / pray most days
- have told a lie / never lied
- would rather listen to music / would rather play music
- read the Bible every day / don't read the Bible every day
- born on an even-numbered day / born on an odd-numbered day
- like pizza more than ice cream / like ice cream more than pizza

Say: **Now, with your eyes closed, slowly raise one arm in front of you and hold out your pointer finger. Let's see how close you are to touching the piece of paper on the wall.** Ask the kids to open their eyes and to stay where they are.

Say: **None of us got to the paper. No one can please God on his or her own either. We've all done wrong things, so we're all sinners and need** help coming to God. But here's the good news: **God wants us to be his friends, no matter what we have or haven't done. No matter what color our hair is or what we like to eat.** Remove the paper from the wall and, as you speak, take it to each of the kids and ask kids to touch it.

Say: **God didn't wait for us to figure out how to get to him. He came to us in the person of Jesus. And Jesus didn't make a set of rules about all the stuff we need to do to be good enough to come to him. He invites everyone—including us—to come to him. He loves us all. Jesus is the only way to God, but he's an open door. We can *all* walk through it and come to God through Jesus.**

CLOSING PRAYER

CIRCLE UP PRAYER
Time: about 2 minutes
Supplies: sheet of paper from the Bible Story

Ask the kids to join you sitting on the floor in a circle. Place the piece of paper they just touched in the middle of the circle. Say: **Jesus is the way, the truth, and the life. He's how we can come to God and be forgiven for all the things we've done wrong. Jesus is the only way to God. Will you say, "Yes, I'll follow Jesus," or "No, I won't follow Jesus"? I've said yes, and I hope you'll say yes too.** Pray: **God, thank you for coming to us in your Son, Jesus. Thank you for loving us and wanting us to be your friend. Help us say yes to you every day. Help us draw closer to you. Amen.**

EXTRA-TIME ACTIVITY—OPTION 1

ONE SIZE FITS ALL?
Time: about 10 minutes
Supplies: none

Join the kids as they sit in a circle on the floor. Explain that, at your signal, each child will toss one shoe into the center of the circle. Kids will then close their eyes and you'll jumble up the shoes.

With their eyes closed, the kids will crawl to the pile of shoes and use their sense of touch—and smell!—to find their own shoe. Ask kids to toss a shoe into the center of the circle and then close their eyes. Then as you jumble up the shoes, toss yours into the mix to help create even more confusion.

Say: **Okay, shoe sniffers. Ready? Go!** Allow kids time to find their shoes—or not—and then have kids discuss:

- **How is finding the one right shoe like Jesus saying he's the only way to God?**
- **How would you explain to a friend what Jesus said?**

Say: **In the game, there was only one right way to play—find your shoe. I'm glad Jesus makes it easier to find him than I made it for you to find your shoe! And I'm glad he's how we come to God!**

EXTRA-TIME ACTIVITY–OPTION 2

INSTANT ARTIST SHOW-AND-TELL
Time: about 10 minutes
Supplies: paper (1 sheet per child), markers

Give a sheet of paper to each child. Say: **Jesus is the way, the truth, and the life. He's the only way to God. So why wouldn't you want people to know about him?**

Ask the kids to create a miniposter about Jesus. Tell them to draw or write things that will help others know who Jesus is. Allow time for kids to work and then let them take turns presenting their posters. Encourage kids to take their posters home and display them where others will see them.

EXTRA-TIME ACTIVITY–OPTION 3

ROAD TRIP!
Time: about 5 minutes
Supplies: sheet of paper, pen

Say: **Jesus said he is the only way to God. And the only way to come to God is to follow Jesus. Here's a question: If you're going to follow Jesus, what does that take and how do you do it?** Discuss and take notes. When the discussion is winding down, read your notes aloud. You'll help kids see what they know already and affirm their answers. Pray aloud for the kids' willingness to be followers of Jesus.

Jesus Said ...

The First Will Be Last

The Point: Serve others.
Scripture Connect: Mark 10:43–45

Supplies for all session 7 activities options: broom, ruler, string, scissors, a deck (or 2) of playing cards, paper, pencils, stopwatch, Bible, clear tape, M&M's, small sandwich bag (or container), plastic spoons (1 per child)

The Basics for Leaders

James and John sidled up beside Jesus and quietly asked for a promotion. When the other ten disciples heard about it, they weren't impressed. In fact, they were indignant.

So Jesus called a quick team meeting. He laid out *exactly* what it took to rise high in his organization: serving others. As in lay-down-your-life-for-others serving others—exactly what his followers saw Jesus living out every day.

That's not how it tends to work in your kids' world. They see talent, self-promotion, and assertiveness nudging some kids to the head of the pack. But serving others? That doesn't seem to contribute much to getting ahead.

You'll help your kids discover the truth of this surprising upside-down kingdom value as you explore what Jesus told his followers then ... and what that means for them now.

OPENING ACTIVITY-OPTION 1

TELL ME THUMBTHING

Time: about 5 minutes, depending on attendance
Supplies: none

After the kids arrive, say: **When people like a movie, they sometimes give it a thumbs-up.** (demonstrate) **If they really like the movie, they give it two thumbs-up. If they dislike or really dislike the movie, they give it one or two thumbs-down.** (demonstrate)

Say: **Please rate how this past week has gone for you. Was it a one or two thumbs-up week? A one or two thumbs-down week? Or maybe you'd give it one thumbs-up and one thumbs-down—it was a good *and* bad week. Rate your week now.**

After kids rate their weeks, give them 30 seconds each to explain why they rated their weeks as they did. You'll go first, sharing a story that models the sort of brief, personal stories you hope kids will share too.

Children will express themselves more over time, and hearing their stories will help you adapt this session to make it even more relevant to your kids' lives.

OPENING ACTIVITY-OPTION 2

HOW LOW CAN YOU GO?

Time: about 10 minutes
Supplies: broom, ruler

Say: **Congratulations! You're all officially entered into the International Limbo League Playoffs!** Explain that limbo is a dance contest in which people pass under a vertical bar—or broom, in this case—with their backs facing the floor. Dancers bend backward and must pass under the bar without touching it, with only their feet touching the floor. The bar is gradually lowered as the contest progresses.

Line the kids up single file and hold the broomstick about six feet from the floor. Make sure everyone can get through the limbo line at least once. Keep lowering the broom each round until you have a champion.

Say: **Jesus said something surprising that reminds me of what we just tried. He said that if you want to be a leader, you have to be a servant.**

If you want to rise high, you have to go low to serve others. This idea surprised his followers at the time, and we're going to explore how that upside-down kingdom principle works in our modern world. But first, a quick game!

Surprising Sayings Game

CARD ASSASSIN

Time: about 15 minutes
Supplies: string, scissors, a deck (or 2) of playing cards

For this activity, simply cut lengths of string and lay them on the floor to create a circle with three zones for players. If you have just a few kids, make the circle no larger than ten feet in diameter. If you have a lot of kids, adjust accordingly.

Give each child ten playing cards. By the way, cards *will* be damaged, so use cheap cards you don't want back. Divide children among the three playing areas. Explain that there are two goals in this game. First, they're trying to flip cards and hit other kids. Second, they're trying not to get hit by cards flipped at them.

Explain the rules:

1. Release cards from within your own playing area—you can't reach across lines.
2. Aim for bodies and not heads.
3. If your card hits someone, call that person's name—it's easy to not notice a card hit you.
4. Keep track of how many times you've been hit.

Play several one-minute rounds, collecting and redistributing cards between rounds. When you've finished playing, gather up the cards and ask kids to discuss:

- What was easiest about this game? What was most challenging?
- If we were to play again, how would you change the rules? Or would you change anything?
- How many times were you hit?

Say: **We have a winner, and it's ___** (name of the child who was hit most often)! Give the winner one card to put in his or her trophy case. Say: **Maybe it seems odd that the person who got hit most often is the winner, but sometimes what we think it takes to win isn't what actually makes us a winner.**

Jesus said that the first will be last. Jesus's disciples got confused about that. Two of them who had decided they wanted to be leaders found out that they didn't know what it took to lead. They didn't know that to faithfully follow Jesus, they had to learn to serve others. Let's find out more.

Surprising Sayings Bible Story

AFFIRMING WORDS

Time: about 15 minutes
Supplies: paper (1 sheet per child), pencils, stopwatch, Bible

Ask the kids to sit in a circle. Give each child a sheet of paper and a pencil and instruct the kids to write their names at the top of their papers. Explain that they will pass around their papers and each child will write an encouraging word or two that describes something good about the person whose name is on the paper.

TIP

If you identified a child at your last session who was willing to read, ask that child to do the honors. Before the kids leave, see if you can rustle up a few more to serve as readers in the future.

Say: **If I were writing on ___'s** (name of a child) **paper, I might write "bright smile" or "very funny." On ___'s paper, I might write "super ideas" or "nice shoes!"** Adapt your examples to fit kids in your group.

Say: **The idea is to write something** *encouraging.* **If you don't know the person well, just describe something you've seen that you like. Maybe it's a bright smile, a great sense of humor, or superior limbo skills. You'll have 20 seconds to write something and then I'll ask you to pass the paper to the left. When our own papers are almost back to us, we will all fold the papers so no one can read what's written there until I give you the signal.**

Start the process—be sure to include your own paper. On each child's paper, write, "A servant." When papers are ready to be passed back to their owners, remember to ask the kids to fold the sheets so there's no peeking. Then have a willing child read Mark 10:43–45 aloud. No volunteers? You can read the passage aloud yourself.

Say: **James and John asked Jesus for leadership positions among the disciples. That's when Jesus called a team meeting and explained what it takes to be a leader in his kingdom. Jesus told the disciples they had to be servants. That's how they would get ahead—by serving others.**

Now, open your paper and see what encouraging words people wrote about you. After kids read what's on their papers, discuss:

- **What did you like most about this activity, encouraging others or being encouraged? Why?**

Say: **I loved both parts. I loved encouraging you and serving you. I also loved having you serve me by encouraging me. I need all the encouragement I can get! It's great if you have a wonderful smile. It's great if you're good at soccer, acting, or limbo dancing.**

But to Jesus, what matters more than any of those is that you're a servant. That you don't put yourself first ... and that's hard to do. It takes noticing others and what they need and then deciding to do something about it. Discuss:

- **Tell us about a time when you saw someone who noticed what others needed and then did something about it.**

Thank kids for sharing. Then say: **Let's serve one another now by praying for one another.**

CLOSING PRAYER

BLESSINGS PRAYER
Time: about 5 minutes
Supplies: none

Have the kids stand. Say: **We'll pray for one another by taking turns blessing one another.** Ask for a volunteer. Stand behind that child, placing your hands on his or her shoulders. Explain that each child will have a turn being prayed for, which involves letting other kids place one hand on the child's shoulder.

If you have a lot of kids, have a few kids put a hand on the child's shoulder and the rest put their hands on the shoulders of those kids touching the child being prayed for.

Explain that you'll start each prayer and end it, but in between, you'd like the kids to add their own prayers out loud. Let them know these prayers don't have to be long or fancy—just brief reasons they thank God for the person being prayed for.

Keep your prayers simple too, along the lines of: **God, thank you for** _____ (child's name). **Please hear us as we pray for** _____. Pause to let kids pray, then conclude with: **Give** _____ **a servant's heart. Amen.**

When finished, close by praying: **God, we love you and want to serve you. Help us serve others too. Amen.**

EXTRA-TIME ACTIVITY—OPTION 1

LARRY, MAY I?

Time: about 10 minutes
Supplies: none

Let the kids take turns leading this version of Mother, May I? Each child leading will use his or her name when suggesting actions. And each action must be a way that kids can serve one another.

For instance, Larry might say, "Larry says, 'Help load the dishwasher,'" or "Larry says, 'Feed your dog.'" Let several kids take turns leading. Discuss:

- **What's something you did last week to serve someone else? How did you feel about it?**
- **How could you serve someone today?**
- **Would you rather serve or be served? Why?**

Say: **It's great to serve others, but Jesus cares more about** *why* **we serve than about our actions. Let's serve because his love is in us rather than just because we're supposed to!**

EXTRA-TIME ACTIVITY—OPTION 2

BENDABLE

Time: about 10 minutes
Supplies: paper (1 sheet per child), clear tape

Roll several sheets of paper into tubes and tape them so they stay in the shape of a cylinder. Use one sheet of paper per child. Once they're taped, set the tubes on the floor so they're sitting upright.

Explain to the kids that this is their chance to do the limbo in reverse—by bending *forward*. Tell them the goal is to bend down, pick up one of the tubes with their teeth without their hands touching the floor, and then stand back up.

When all kids who want to try have had an opportunity, continue by saying: **In some cultures, it's a sign of respect to bow, to bend forward. The more you respect someone, the deeper your bow.** Discuss:

- **Who would be worthy of such a deep bow? Why do you respect that person so much?**
- **In what ways can you serve others by showing them respect?**

Say: **Being respectful is one way we can serve others. That's good, because we know that Jesus wants us to serve others.**

EXTRA-TIME ACTIVITY—OPTION 3

OPEN WIDE

Time: about 5 minutes
Supplies: M&M's, small sandwich bags (or containers), plastic spoons (1 per child)

Before the kids arrive, place nine candies in a small sandwich bag. You'll need one bag for every three kids. Have kids form groups of three and sit knee to knee with their partners. Give each child a plastic spoon and give every group a candy bag.

Tell the kids they're about to get snacks—maybe. It all depends on them serving others and being served in return. In each group, the child whose birthday is closest to June 23 (that's the United Nations Public Service Day), will serve as the snack master first.

The snack master is the only person in each group who'll keep his eyes open. His job is to use his voice to guide the snack giver to getting a single M&M on a spoon and then getting the spoon into the mouth of the snack getter. Say: **The snack master will serve your group by helping the snack** giver get three pieces of candy into the mouth of the snack getter. Both the snack giver and snack getter must keep their eyes closed and rely on directions from the snack master.

Make sure the groups switch roles so everyone gets to be the snack master, snack giver, and snack getter. Say: **Thanks for serving one another—that was fun! Even though serving others isn't always that much fun, it's what Jesus wants us to do.**

Jesus Said ...

Put Me First

The Point: Love Jesus most of all.
Scripture Connect: Matthew 10:37–39

Supplies for all session 8 activities options: soft baby doll, clear glass jar, several stones, rice, bowl, Bible, paper clips (1 per child)

The Basics for Leaders

When Jesus says that if we don't love him more than our parents and children, we're not worthy of him, it's easy to picture Jesus wagging a finger at his followers and scowling. He sounds severe, as if he's trying to push people away.

But he's not forcing his followers to love either their families or him. He's not saying to quit loving those closest to us. Rather, he's saying to love him most—and for good reason.

It's in loving Jesus that we give up clinging to life and then find new life in him. A life fueled by love and commitment. A life that empowers us to love our families in deeper, richer ways.

Jesus asks—demands—that we love him more than anything and anyone else. And that's a kingdom truth you'll help kids explore in this session.

OPENING ACTIVITY–OPTION 1

TELL ME THUMBTHING
Time: about 5 minutes, depending on attendance
Supplies: none

After the kids arrive, say: **When people like a movie, they sometimes give it a thumbs-up.** (demonstrate) **If they really like the movie, they give it two thumbs-up. If they dislike or really dislike the movie, they give it one or two thumbs-down.** (demonstrate)

Say: **Please rate how this past week has gone for you. Was it a one or two thumbs-up week? A one or two thumbs-down week? Or maybe you'd give it one thumbs-up and one thumbs-down—it was a good *and* bad week. Rate your week now.**

After kids rate their weeks, give them 30 seconds each to explain why they rated their weeks as they did. You'll go first, sharing a story that models the sort of brief, personal stories you hope kids will share too.

Children will express themselves more over time, and hearing their stories will help you adapt this session to make it even more relevant to your kids' lives.

OPENING ACTIVITY—OPTION 2

FIRST ON MY LIST

Time: about 10 minutes
Supplies: none

Say: **You're about to be left alone on a deserted island. Not really, but it *might* happen, so it's good to be prepared. The good news is there's plenty of food, water, and shelter on the island. The bad news is there's nothing else there unless you bring it.**

Tell the kids they'll each get to take three must-have items with them. The three objects can be anything, except people. Form pairs and let the kids talk over what they'd bring. After a few minutes, ask them to share their lists with the larger group, explaining why they chose what they did.

Say: **Some belongings are more important than others. And some *people* matter more to us than others. I say that not to be mean but because it's true.**

Jesus had something surprising to say about that. He told his followers that when it came to people, *he* had to come first. To follow him, we need to love Jesus most of all. We'll take a look at what he meant and how Jesus took his own advice. But first, let's play a game!

Surprising Sayings **Game**

BABY CATCH

Time: about 15 minutes
Supplies: soft baby doll

Ask the kids to stand in a circle and number off—each kid needs a unique number. Say: **I'm certifying you all as best ever babysitters. And because you're so well trained, I know I can trust you with little Bailey here.** Show the children the baby doll.

Say: **Imagine this: You show up for babysitting duty and I've come to the front door to let you in. You look up, and there's Bailey in a third-floor window. Because Bailey loves you, she wants to see you right away and crawls out the window. It's up to you to save her.**

Tell the kids that you'll call out a number as you toss the doll high in the air. It's up to whoever has that number to catch the doll. Repeat the activity until every child has had an opportunity to catch the doll. Once or twice, repeat a number—the child with that number will be caught off guard. At least once, call out a number that no child has—just to see what happens. Ask: **Had you really been in this situation, what would have been more important than saving Bailey's life? Would you have stopped to send a text or play a video game?**

Say: **In life, some things just come first. You drop everything for what's most important to you—for** *who's* **most important to you. When Jesus told his followers that** *he* **expected to come first in their lives and that they should love** *him* **most of all, I think they were probably surprised. Let's listen to what he said to them ... and what this means for us.**

Surprising Sayings **Bible Story**

WHO'S ON FIRST?

Time: about 15 minutes
Supplies: clear glass jar, several stones, rice, bowl, Bible

Show children the clear jar. Say: **Some people say our hearts are like this jar. We care about a lot of stuff, but there's not enough room for us to care about everything.** Hold up a stone. **For me, one big thing I care about**

is my family. Place the stone in the jar and then hold up a second stone. **What about you? What are some big things you care about?** For each answer, put a stone in the jar. Some possible answers might be pets, school, health, God, and friends.

Those are some great things to care about. Hold up the rice. **Then there are things you care about, but they're not all that important**. Pour a bit of rice into the jar. **Washing the dishes—I do it, but I don't really care that much about it. What about you?** As kids call out small things they care about, add rice until the jar is full.

Slightly shaking the jar as you add rice will help fill the spaces between stones.

Say: **That's a full heart. Big stuff to care about, small stuff to care about—and it all fits**. Pour the contents of the jar into a bowl. Set the stones aside.

Say: **Watch what happens when we fill the jar starting with the small things**. Pour the rice into the jar and then try to add back the stones—they won't all fit. **The big stuff doesn't fit! There's no room for us to care about the big things when we care about all the little things instead.**

Jesus understood this—and he had something surprising to say about it. Ask a willing child to read Matthew 10:37–38 aloud. No volunteers? You can read the passage aloud yourself.

Say: **Jesus says that *he* wants to come first when we're thinking about who and what we care about. He doesn't just want it—he expects it. Actually … he *demands* it. He says that he's got to fit in our jar—our life—before anything else is added.** Ask: **Why do you think Jesus said that?**

Thank kids for sharing and then point out what Jesus *didn't* say: **He didn't say that nothing else can go in our jars. We can still care about pets and pizza. We can still love our families and friends. We just have to love Jesus most of all. And Jesus didn't just tell us to put God before family; he did it himself.**

Say: **Jesus was busy teaching and healing people when his earthly family showed up. Listen to what happened.** Read Mark 3:31–33 aloud, then explain: **Jesus put doing God's will first and said that those who do the same are his family. That doesn't mean he didn't love his mother; it meant he was doing what he wants us to do. We are to put Jesus first and love him most of all.**

CLOSING PRAYER

SHAPING ME

Time: about 5 minutes
Supplies: paper clips (1 per child)

Give each child a paper clip. Say: **Look at your paper clip, and you'll see it's just a thin piece of metal that's running in circles. It heads one way, doubles back, and then does the same thing again. Kind of like us.**

We tell Jesus we'll follow him and put him first, but then we forget. We get busy. We do other things. Please straighten out your paper clips. Demonstrate, warning the kids to be careful so they don't poke themselves. Then ask them to bend their paper clips into the shape of a heart. When finished, ask the kids to hold their paper clip hearts in their hands.

Say: **Putting Jesus first and loving him most of all isn't something that happens all at once. We have to decide to do it every day. And it's all about our hearts turning to Jesus.**

Ask kids to hold their paper clip hearts as you pray: **Jesus, thank you for your endless love, for loving us before we ever loved you. Help us love you and follow you today and every day. Change our hearts, Jesus. Help us love you most of all. Amen.**

EXTRA-TIME ACTIVITY—OPTION 1

SPELL IT OUT

Time: about 10 minutes
Supplies: none

Have the kids form pairs and tell them that they're going to take turns spelling out words on one another's backs. Say: **When you're writing, you can't say the letters out loud, so write clearly in capital letters. When someone's writing on your back, the only thing you can say is, "Repeat, please," if you can't tell what was spelled out. You'll take turns writing whatever word you'd use to complete a sentence.** Tell the kids to take ten seconds to decide who'll be the first writer in each pair.

After the kids are in position, say the following sentences, allowing time for them to write. Ask those children who are "reading" to tell their partners what they thought was written on their backs. After confirming what was actually written, have the kids switch roles and answer the same question. Here are some example sentences:

- My first choice for an ice cream flavor is …
- My first choice for a pizza topping is …
- The movie I love most of all is …
- If I were going on a trip, my first choice would be to go to …
- My first choice for a vegetable is …

Thank the kids for playing, then say: **We make a lot of choices about what's first in our lives. Let's make the best choice—to put Jesus first and love him most of all!**

EXTRA-TIME ACTIVITY—OPTION 2

RAH-RAH-RIFFIC
Time: about 10 minutes
Supplies: none

Split the kids into teams. If you have only a few kids, divide them into pairs. Say: **Thank you for coming to cheerleader tryouts. Your job is to come up with a cheer that helps everyone know that Jesus is number one. That's the message, but you can use whatever words you want. Extra points for coming up with actions too!**

Send groups to different parts of the room so they can brainstorm and rehearse. Then call them back so each team can demonstrate its cheer. Applaud the cheers and be affirming. Say: **Congratulations, you all made the team! Even better, if you do what you've just cheered—if you put Jesus first and love him most of all—you'll make another team: the Jesus followers! Go team!**

EXTRA-TIME ACTIVITY—OPTION 3

NO, NO, AFTER YOU
Time: about 5 minutes
Supplies: none

Gather the kids by a door and say: **Sometimes we show respect for people by opening the door for them. But what if there are two people at the door at the very same time and each wants to let the other person go first? How would they convince the other person to go first?**

Pair up a few kids and tell them that their mission is to come up with reasons the other person should go through the door first. They'll each need good reasons and enough reasons so the other person finally gives in. Here's an opportunity for your quick-on-their-feet kids to shine. Tap them for the first round and then ask if there are volunteers who also want to give it a try.

Say: **Here's the good news when it comes to putting Jesus first: we know we need to do it, and he knows we need to do it, so there won't be any arguing when we decide to put Jesus first.** Ask: **What's an area of your life in which you need to put Jesus first?**

Say: **Jesus said to put him first and to love him most of all. He also said that when we do that, we don't lose out—we actually find new life. Let's decide to take Jesus at his word and put him first!**

Jesus Said ...
Fish for People

The Point: You have good news to share.
Scripture Connect: Matthew 4:18–20

Supplies for all session 9 activities options: paper, scissors, markers, newspaper, masking tape (or painters' tape), stopwatch, Bible, paper plates

The Basics for Leaders

For many Christians, sharing the good news about Jesus is scary. We think it involves reciting Bible verses and defending the faith as hostile critics pepper us with questions. No wonder so many of us keep our heads down and say nothing. Yes, we have good news to share, but people will have to pry it out of us.

But what if our good news is less about Bible facts and more about sharing our own story–about sharing what Jesus has done for us and how we've changed? Our own stories don't require defending because they're *our stories*. We're simply reporting what happened when Jesus touched our lives.

In this session, you'll help the children discover that they have good news to share. It's good news about Jesus but also good news about what Jesus has done for them. You'll help them put their story into words and be ready to go fishin'!

OPENING ACTIVITY–OPTION 1

TELL ME THUMBTHING
Time: about 5 minutes, depending on attendance
Supplies: none

After the kids arrive, say: **When people like a movie, they sometimes give it a thumbs-up.** (demonstrate) **If they really like the movie, they give it two thumbs-up. If they dislike or really dislike the movie, they give it one or two thumbs-down.** (demonstrate)

Say: **Please rate how this past week has gone for you. Was it a one or two thumbs-up week? A one or two thumbs-down week? Or maybe you'd give it one thumbs-up and one thumbs-down—it was a good *and* bad week. Rate your week now.**

After kids rate their weeks, give them 30 seconds each to explain why they rated their weeks as they did. You'll go first, sharing a story that models the sort of brief, personal stories you hope kids will share too.

Children will express themselves more over time, and hearing their stories will help you adapt this session to make it even more relevant to your kids' lives.

OPENING ACTIVITY—OPTION 2

FLYING FISH

Time: about 10 minutes
Supplies: paper (1 sheet per child), scissors, markers, newspapers

Give each child a sheet of paper and scissors. Have kids cut out the shape of a large fish. They should also write their names on their fish. Line kids up side by side about twenty feet from a wall. Tell them to face the wall and lay their fish on the floor in front of them.

Say: **It may not look like it, but that wall in front of you is the ocean, and if your fish is going to survive, you've got to get it back into water.**

TIP

This activity works best on a tile floor, but if you're on carpet, you can easily make it work by having kids slightly crumple their fish before placing them on the floor.

You'll do that by waving a section of newspaper behind your fish.

Give each child a section of newspaper. Say: **You can't touch your fish in any way—your fish must be carried by the wind you make with the newspaper all the way to the ocean. Start flapping!** If some kids struggle to get their fish moving, ask those who finish early to help others.

When the children have finished, collect the newspapers and say: **Back when Jesus was on earth, he was around fish and fishermen. And He said something about fishing that was surprising. We'll take a look at what he said after we play a quick game!**

Surprising Sayings Game

GIDDYUP GET THERE

Time: about 15 minutes
Supplies: masking tape (or painters' tape), stopwatch

Say: **I have good news, and I want to tell others as quickly as possible. If you had good news to share and wanted to deliver it to someone fast, you might try these methods.**

Explain to the kids that they're all on the same team. They will run a relay twice—competing against the clock, not one another. Encourage kids to cheer one another on. Use tape to create a starting line and another line 15 feet away; kids will race to that line and back again.

Give each child a different way to move—that's the fun in this relay. And if you have just a few kids, it's okay to have each child run the relay several times in different ways. Just keep the number of laps consistent from round one to round two. Here are some examples of ways the kids can run the relay:

- gallop like horses
- waddle like penguins
- walk like crabs (on hands and feet, facing up toward the ceiling)
- walk like bridesmaids (step, pause)
- slither like snakes
- walk backward
- skip
- walk with toe-to-heel steps
- leap like ballerinas
- walk sideways
- hop like kangaroos

Say: **Let's see how fast you can run the Giddyup Get There races!** Tell the first child how he or she will move and then say: **Ready? Go!** Start the stopwatch.

Run the relay twice, comparing the time it took to complete the relay. When running it the second time, use the same list of movements but let different kids do them. Discuss:

- **Which way was the easiest to move in a hurry? Which was the hardest? Why?**
- **Tell us about a time when you had to get someplace in a hurry. What happened?**

After letting several kids share their stories, continue by saying: **Before we started our relay, I talked about having good news to share. But you didn't ask me** *what* **good news I was talking about. If you're going to go to the trouble of hopping, leaping, and crab walking, don't you want to know what message you have to deliver? We'll get to what the good news is, but first, let's join some people who are being asked to deliver good news. And they're being asked to do it in a very surprising way!**

Surprising Sayings Bible Story

FISHY FOLLOWING

Time: about 20 minutes
Supplies: Bible

Ask the kids to sit on the floor in a circle. Read Matthew 4:18–20 aloud. Then ask for three volunteers. Place two volunteers (Simon and Andrew) inside the circle and the third volunteer (Jesus) outside the circle. Tell the children that they will silently act out the actions you describe.

Say: **Those of us in the audience have a part to play too: we're fish. Show me your best fish face.** (pause as kids do as you've asked) **Perfect! Now we're ready to begin!**

One day, Jesus was walking along the shore of the Sea of Galilee, which was actually a lake. (indicate that Jesus should walk slowly around the circle) **But people called it a sea because it was a really, really big lake. Two guys, who made their living fishing, were busy throwing their nets into the water.** (pause for some net-throwing action) **There was Simon—wave, Simon!** (pause) **And also Andrew. Wave, Andrew!** (pause)

Just beyond the nets were fish. Fish, make fish faces! (pause) **There were a lot of fish! Jesus stopped where Simon and Andrew could see**

him. (pause) **They probably waved to Jesus because they'd seen him around. Jesus probably waved back, and then he said something very interesting: "Come follow me, and I'll teach you how to fish for people."** **Simon looked at Andrew.** (pause) **Andrew looked at Simon.** (pause) **They both looked at Jesus.** (pause) **The fish looked at the nets, which were no longer in the water.** (pause)

Then Simon and Andrew did something the fish had never seen them do: they walked away from their nets and followed Jesus. (pause) **The fish** *loved* **seeing the fishermen walk away from the water, so they slapped their fins together in applause!** (pause) **Thank you, actors!** Ask everyone to sit in a circle and discuss:

- **What do you think Jesus meant when he said Simon and Andrew would fish for people?**
- **Fishing for people is part of our job as Jesus followers too. How do we do that?**

Tell the kids that many followers of Jesus don't talk about him much. Say: **Some people are afraid to talk about Jesus because they don't know much about the Bible. Or they don't think they're qualified because they still do wrong things.**

But you don't have to be perfect to talk about Jesus. And you don't have to know everything about the Bible. We can share who Jesus is, how Jesus has helped and changed us, and that Jesus is a friend who also wants to be friends with everyone. That's the good news we can share!

Ask everyone to find a partner. Find a partner yourself; you'll model what to say as you tell your own faith story. Keep it short and age-appropriate for your kids. Tell your partner who Jesus is: the Son of God who loves us. Tell your partner how knowing Jesus has helped you. For example, maybe you used to be afraid all the time but now you're not. Tell your partner that Jesus is your friend and wants to be your partner's friend too.

Lead kids in sharing their stories with their partners. Begin with the person in each pair who's sitting closest to you. Keep in mind that you might have children who are not yet Jesus followers. That's okay; they'll hear a faith story in this activity.

Walk kids through repeating who Jesus is, what change he's made in their lives, and saying that Jesus wants to be friends with everyone. Then the kids can switch roles. When they're finished, say: **That's how you fish for people. You tell them about Jesus and who he is in your life. Now let's ask Jesus to give us opportunities to share our faith stories with others.**

CLOSING PRAYER

STORY THANKS

Time: about 1 minute
Supplies: none

Ask the kids to sit with their hands in front of them, palms up. Pray: **Thank you, Lord, for loving us and for giving us a faith story. We gratefully accept everything you give us.** Then ask the kids to turn their palms so they're facing out. Continue: **Lord, please give us the opportunity to share our stories with others. We want others to know you too. We know we have good news to share—good news about you. Amen.**

EXTRA-TIME ACTIVITY–OPTION 1

MUMBLE BUMBLE

Time: about 10 minutes
Supplies: none

Say: **Sometimes when we want to share good news with others, we don't know what to say. In those cases, we might not say anything or we might mumble.** Have the kids sit in a circle. Tell them to practice mumbling by sucking their lips in and acting as if they have no teeth. The goal is to talk about their favorite pizza toppings without letting anyone see their teeth. If a child shows his or her teeth while talking, that child is not going to be the champion mumbler.

Turn to a child next to you and tell him or her what you like on a pizza. Go around the circle and see how many kids can mumble about their favorite pizza toppings. When you've made it around the circle, say: **I don't think any of us will get trophies for mumbling—but that's a good thing. We have good news to share!** Discuss: **What's the best way to share the good news about Jesus—through what we say, what we do, or something else? Why?**

EXTRA-TIME ACTIVITY-OPTION 2

TURN THAT FROWN UPSIDE DOWN?

Time: about 10 minutes
Supplies: paper plates, markers (or pencils)

Give each child a paper plate and a marker. Ask the kids to draw a big smile on their plates. Then have them turn their plates upside down—now it's a frown. Explain that you'll be reading some two-part situations. Kids will show with their plates whether they think what you say is good news (a smile) or bad news (a frown). Be sure to pause before reading the second part of each situation:

- You got the flu ... which kept you from going on a fun field trip.
- You got the hiccups ... while playing hide and seek.
- You were invited to a friend's party ... and had a great time.
- You did a perfect dive off the high board ... but you can't swim.
- You love your new trampoline ... if only you hadn't fallen off and broken an arm.
- You crashed your skateboard into the curb and fell ... but that kept you from zipping in front of a speeding truck.
- You found a 100-dollar bill on the street ... then lost it on the way home.
- You found a penny on the street ... and you discovered that it's worth 1,000 dollars.

Say: **Sometimes things happen that seem great, but they really aren't. And sometimes things happen that aren't so great, but they're good in the end. Here's something that's** *always* **good—the good news you can share about Jesus. Jesus wants you to go fishing for others by sharing the good news!**

EXTRA-TIME ACTIVITY-OPTION 3

GOOD-NEWS STORY STRETCHER

Time: about 5 minutes
Supplies: none

The goal of this game is to turn bad news into good news—three words at a time! Tell the kids that you'll start by saying some bad news. Their job, as they go around the circle, is to add three words that turn the bad news into good news.

Here are some story launches you can use:

- **When Jacob slammed his fingers in the door ...**
- **Olivia wasn't just mad; she was furious because ...**
- **Flunking the test was a bad thing for Michael because ...**
- **After the bullies cornered Kaitlyn, the biggest bully said ...**
- **Jesus told Simon and Andrew, "You won't make money fishing for fish anymore, but ..."**

Say: **Simon and Andrew had good news to share about Jesus—that's why they fished for people. You have good news about Jesus to share too, so get fishing!**

Jesus Said ...
Forgive and
Keep Forgiving

The Point: Forgive—and forgive again.
Scripture Connect: Matthew 18:21–35

Supplies for all session 10 activities options: paper, pencils, Bible, coins (1 per child), colored pencils, safety pins, plastic spoons, cotton balls

The Basics for Leaders

How important is forgiveness? Well, if you ever intend to see heaven, it's one of the most important things you can have. Without forgiveness, without grace, you have no hope. God's forgiveness is essential.

But what about that *other* forgiveness—the kind that you can give to others? If Jesus is to be believed, it's just as important.

In this session, your kids (and you) will grapple with the connection Jesus made between how we forgive others and how God will forgive us. It's an awkward, surprising thing for Jesus to say, maybe even a bit scary. Because if he's serious, it means we've got some work to do.

OPENING ACTIVITY-OPTION 1

TELL ME THUMBTHING
Time: about 5 minutes, depending on attendance
Supplies: none

After the kids arrive, say: **When people like a movie, they sometimes give it a thumbs-up.** (demonstrate) **If they really like the movie, they give it two thumbs-up. If they dislike or really dislike the movie, they give it one or two thumbs-down.** (demonstrate)

Say: **Please rate how this past week has gone for you. Was it a one or two thumbs-up week? A one or two thumbs-down week? Or maybe you'd give it one thumbs-up and one thumbs-down—it was a good** and **bad week. Rate your week now.**

After kids rate their weeks, give them 30 seconds each to explain why they rated their weeks as they did. You'll go first, sharing a story that models the sort of brief, personal stories you hope kids will share too.

Children will express themselves more over time, and hearing their stories will help you adapt this session to make it even more relevant to your kids' lives.

OPENING ACTIVITY-OPTION 2

FORGIVENESS CIRCLE

Time: about 10 minutes
Supplies: paper (3 sheets per child), pencils

Give each child three pieces of paper and a pencil. Say: **There's a story told about a famous Italian painter named Giotto. He wanted to show how skilled he was as a painter, but instead of painting a person or landscape, he painted a perfect circle. Giotto figured that proved he could paint anything.**

Tell kids you want them to do what Giotto did: draw a perfect circle that fills most of a sheet of paper. Ask them to use their nondominant hand, the one they don't use to write. Allow up to thirty seconds for the kids to draw and then ask them to hold up their circles for inspection.

Say: **Hmm … they're not perfect, but I forgive you. Maybe if your pencils were closer to your brains, where you're** *picturing* **a perfect circle, it would help.** Ask the kids to hold their pencils in their mouths and lean over to draw a circle on their second piece of paper. After they're done, ask them to hold up their circles for inspection. Say: **Still not per-fect, but I forgive you again for letting me down.**

On their third sheet of paper, tell the kids to use their dominant hand to draw a circle. When they've finished, have them hold up papers for inspection. Say: **Much better, but still not perfect. But once again, I forgive you.** Discuss: **How many tries do you think you'd need before you could draw an absolutely perfect circle?** Allow kids to respond.

Say: **Even if I gave you 490 tries, your drawing probably wouldn't be perfect. If we looked close enough, we'd find some flaw in every circle you drew. If I expect you to do something that you just can't do, you're sure to let me down.**

Jesus had something surprising to say about dealing with people who let us down. We'll find out what that was after a quick game!

Surprising Sayings Game

MATH MASTERS

Time: about 15 minutes
Supplies: none

Have the kids get into pairs and stand facing each other. Explain that this game requires the ability to count quickly. Kids will place their hands behind their backs and hold up at least two fingers on each hand. Then, at your signal, they'll hold their hands in front of them, fingers still extended, so their partner can see how many total fingers are being held up.

In each pair, whoever calls out the correct total of fingers being held up on all *four* hands first is the winner. Demonstrate the game with a volunteer. Let the kids play a few rounds and then reconfigure them so they're playing in groups of three and then groups of four. You can even play as a whole group! When kids have finished playing, discuss:

- **What made this game easy? What made it hard?**
- **Tell us about something you've had to do over and over again even though you didn't want to do it again.**

Say: **There's something Jesus said that we're to keep doing over and over, even though we usually don't want to do it. It's forgiving others. Let's hear more about what Jesus said.**

Surprising Sayings Bible Story

SHOW ME THE MONEY!

Time: about 15 minutes
Supplies: Bible, coins (1 per child)

One great thing about a lot of Jesus's parables is that kids can act them out. Ask for four volunteers. If you have just a few kids, you can play the role of the king or queen if necessary.

Say: **Jesus told a lot of parables, or stories, that had deeper truths tucked inside. Sometimes he explained what that deeper truth was, and sometimes he let people figure it out for themselves. Let's see if we can spot the deeper truth in this parable.**

Explain that your volunteers will silently act out the story as it unfolds. However, because there's violence in the story, they're not allowed to actually throttle or beat one another. The rest of the kids will provide brief sound effects during the big prison punishment scene.

Place the king on one side and debtor number one and debtor number two on the other side. If possible, use a child-friendly translation of the Bible to read Matthew 18:21–35 aloud. Pause after describing an action taken by one of the characters to allow actors to do what you described. When you've finished reading, thank your actors and sound-effects experts. Discuss:

- **What do you think was Jesus's point in this parable?**
- **Which character reminds you most of yourself? Why?**
- **How do you feel hearing that God will forgive you in the same way you forgive others?**

Say: **Forgiveness is so important to Jesus that he came to die on a cross so, through him, we could be forgiven for our sins. So maybe it shouldn't be a surprise that Jesus wants us to learn to forgive too—to pass on to others the same forgiveness that we receive from God. And Jesus doesn't just suggest we forgive others; he demands it. If we want to be forgiven, we've got to forgive others. We're to forgive again and again.**

Give each child a coin. Ask the kids to look at the head on the front of their coins. Say: **Please picture the face of someone you need to forgive,** someone who hurt you in some way or made fun of you. (pause) **Now remember how you felt when this person hurt you or made fun of you. (pause) Maybe you have every right to get even with this person. But Jesus asks you to forgive the person.**

Forgiving doesn't mean you have to trust the person or pretend what happened didn't happen, but it does mean that you give up your right to hurt them back. It means you don't wish the other person harm. In a few moments, we'll pray together. For now, keep holding your coin and picturing a person you might need to forgive.

CLOSING PRAYER

CARRY IT TO THE CROSS

Time: about 3 minutes
Supplies: sheet of paper, coins from the Bible Story

Without talking, take a sheet of paper and tear it so it becomes a cross. Lay the cross on the floor where the kids can see it.

Say: **When I see a cross, I'm reminded that Jesus paid a price so I could be forgiven. I'm a sinner—I've done wrong things and I still do wrong things. The price for that is to never be close to God. But because Jesus gave himself on the cross to pay for my sins, I can be forgiven and be a friend of God's.**

Maybe I can do the same for someone who hurts me. I can say, "I won't demand the person pay for what he or she did." I can just let it go. I can forgive.

Tell the kids to close their eyes. Say: **As I pray, you can decide if you want to forgive the person you have in mind who hurt you. Maybe you're not ready to do that yet, and that's okay—forgiveness can take a while. But if you are ready, lay your coin on the cross. Decide not to hold a grudge. Decide to forgive—and forgive again.**

Pray: **God, thank you for forgiving us through what Jesus did on the cross. He didn't deserve to pay for our sins, but he paid for them anyway. You didn't have to forgive us, but you did. Give us hearts that are as forgiving as yours. Amen.**

EXTRA-TIME ACTIVITY-OPTION 1

WEARABLE FORGIVENESS

Time: about 10 minutes
Supplies: paper (2 sheets per child), pencils, colored pencils, safety pins

Give each child two sheets of paper and a pencil. Explain that the kids are all now officially part of your T-shirt design team. Their job is to take no more than five minutes to design a T-shirt about forgiveness. They can draw something, write something, or combine both a drawing and words in a design. They can sketch out their design ideas on one sheet of paper and then do a final design on the other sheet.

Say: **You've got just five minutes to come up with a design. Ready? Get designing!** Let the kids know when four minutes have passed so they can finish up their final designs. After five minutes, have kids present their designs and then, using safety pins, attach the designs to kids' shirts. Say: **It's good to be reminded about forgiveness because it's incredibly important to Jesus. He says to forgive—and forgive again.**

EXTRA-TIME ACTIVITY-OPTION 2

ZEROES ON PARADE

Time: about 5 minutes
Supplies: paper, pencils

Give each child a pencil and a sheet of paper. Say: **When Jesus said to forgive 77 times (or 490 times, depending on the translation), He isn't saying to forgive someone a certain amount of times and then stop forgiving. He's making a point: we're to forgive and keep forgiving.**

But while we're talking about how often to forgive, can you think of a number that's so big, you'd stop forgiving a person after you'd reached it? Let's try writing some big numbers! Tell the kids you'll call out some big numbers. They're to write down those numbers and then tell you how many zeroes are in each.

- **one thousand** (three zeroes)
- **one billion** (nine zeroes)
- **one hundred** (two zeroes)

- **one trillion** (12 zeroes)
- **one decillion** (33 zeroes)
- **one undecillion** (36 zeroes)
- **ten** (just one zero)

Say: **Before we finish today, consider how long it would take to write one centillion—that's 303 zeroes! Save that one for when you get home. Jesus never intended his followers to keep track of how often they forgive. Instead, he's asking us to do what he does: forgive—and keep on forgiving!**

EXTRA-TIME ACTIVITY—OPTION 3

FORGIVEN RELAY RACE

Time: about 10 minutes
Supplies: plastic spoons, cotton balls

Form kids into two teams of equal size. You can join in to even up the teams if needed. Establish a starting line and a wall that will be the halfway point. Explain that in this relay race, runners will carry a cotton ball on a spoon. They'll touch the wall, turn, and hurry back to the starting line. That's when they'll hand off the spoon and cotton ball to a teammate.

Say: **You can't touch the cotton ball in any way—it has to stay on the spoon. If you drop it, you have to pick it up and ask your opposing runner to forgive you for dropping it. You can't move on until the other player says, "I forgive you."**

Here's what's tricky: If you don't forgive others, they won't forgive you. If you wait to forgive them, they may wait a *very* **long time to forgive you. Forgive or don't forgive—it's up to you.** Launch the relay race. When it's over, discuss:

- **How fair do you think Jesus was being when he said that if we want to be forgiven, we'd have to forgive others?**
- **Why is it so hard to forgive others? What might make it easier?**

Thank kids for sharing their thoughts. Then say: **Whether you found forgiving others easy or hard, Jesus still calls his followers to do this: forgive—and keep on forgiving!**

Jesus Said ...
With Faith, Nothing Is Impossible

The Point: Have faith in God.

Scripture Connect: Matthew 17:20–21

Supplies for all session 11 activities options: paper, pencils, Bible, mustard seeds, envelopes, pen, individually wrapped candy (3 pieces per child), stopwatch

The Basics for Leaders

Jesus's followers have used what he said in Matthew 17:20–21 to beat themselves up for 2,000 years. When there's a stubborn problem that can't be solved, we're often quick to think, "If I just had more faith, I could beat this thing. After all, Jesus said I should be able to move mountains."

But "moving mountains" was a saying at the time that meant "doing what's almost impossible." And we forget that in whom we *place* our faith is more important than the amount of that faith. Having faith in God and relying on him—that's what really matters.

As you discuss this surprising saying of Jesus—that with faith, nothing is impossible—be sure your kids don't leave thinking that it's up to them to solve their most difficult problems alone. The answer to the troubling times in their lives isn't doubling down and working harder to believe but coming wholeheartedly to God, who can help them.

OPENING ACTIVITY-OPTION 1

TELL ME THUMBTHING

Time: about 5 minutes, depending on attendance
Supplies: none

After the kids arrive, say: **When people like a movie, they sometimes give it a thumbs-up.** (demonstrate) **If they really like the movie, they give it two thumbs-up. If they dislike or really dislike the movie, they give it one or two thumbs-down.** (demonstrate)

Say: **Please rate how this past week has gone for you. Was it a one or two thumbs-up week? A one or two thumbs-down week? Or maybe you'd give it one thumbs-up and one thumbs-down—it was a good *and* bad week. Rate your week now.**

After kids rate their weeks, give them 30 seconds each to explain why they rated their weeks as they did. You'll go first, sharing a story that models the sort of brief, personal stories you hope kids will share too.

Children will express themselves more over time, and hearing their stories will help you adapt this session to make it even more relevant to your kids' lives.

OPENING ACTIVITY-OPTION 2

IMPOSSIBLE ART SHOW-AND-TELL

Time: about 10 minutes
Supplies: paper (1 sheet per child), pencils

Give each child a sheet of paper and a pencil. Say, **On your paper, draw something impossible. Maybe it's a man with 42 legs or a waterfall where the water flows up. What you draw is up to you, but make sure it's impossible.** Allow time for kids to draw and then have them present their drawings to the larger group.

Say: **You know, there are a lot of things that people once thought were impossible that turned out to be possible. It was once impossible to talk to someone on the other side of the country, to walk on the moon, and to do organ transplants.**

Choose one of the kids' drawings and ask: **So how might we make what's in this picture possible? What would it take?** Lead kids in brainstorming how to turn the impossible into something possible. If there's time, tackle several drawings.

Say: **What we just did is what lots of people do: we relied on ourselves to try to make the impossible possible. And maybe with enough work and creativity, we could do it. But what if I said that there's one thing you could do that makes *anything* possible? That's a surprising thing to say—but Jesus said it. We'll talk about what He said, but first, let's play a quick game!**

Surprising Sayings Game

CHOO CHOO ADVENTURE

Time: about 15 minutes
Supplies: none

Divide the kids into groups of three, then ask each group to line up single file. Have the last two kids in each group put their hands on the shoulders of the kid in front of them. Say: **Your group is now a train. If you're first in line, you're the engine. If you're second in line, you're the coal car. If you're last in line, you're the caboose.**

Explain that at your signal, engines and coal cars will shut their eyes and keep them closed. Only cabooses will have their eyes open, and they'll silently direct their train by squeezing the shoulders of the coal cars, who'll then squeeze the shoulders of the engine. If the train should turn left, the caboose should squeeze the coal car's left shoulder. Right turn? Squeeze the right shoulder. Slow or stop? Pull back gently on both shoulders. Go? A gentle push on both shoulders.

Say: **Your trains will now go on a journey. Your goal is to touch the nose of your engine to each wall and then choo choo on back to where you're now standing. Of course, do it without crashing into walls or other trains. Engines, no putting your hands out front of you—you've got to have faith in your caboose. Ditto for you, coal cars. There are no blindfolds because I'm trusting you to keep your eyes closed.**

Tell everyone but cabooses to close their eyes. Say: **Tackle the walls in any order you want. Start now!** After trains have made their journeys, discuss:

- Overall, how do you think your train did?
- Which was the best spot: engine, coal car, or caboose? Why?
- What helped you have faith in your caboose?

Say: **Jesus said something surprising about having faith. Let's hear what he said.**

Surprising Sayings Bible Story

MUSTARD SEED FAITH

Time: about 15 minutes
Supplies: Bible, mustard seeds, envelopes

Say: **A man brought his son to Jesus's disciples for healing, but they couldn't help the boy. So the man went to Jesus, who had no problem healing the boy. Later, the disciples asked Jesus why they couldn't heal the boy. Let's hear how Jesus answered.**

> **TIP**
> If you identified a child at your last session who was willing to read, ask that child to do the honors. Before the kids leave, see if you can rustle up few more to serve as readers in the future.

Ask a willing child to read Matthew 17:20–21 aloud. No volunteers? You can read the passage aloud yourself.

Say: **Jesus had been training the disciples for a few years. Because of Jesus's power, the disciples had been able to help people in the past. But not this time.**

In a minute, I'll ask you to find a partner and tell that person about a time when you thought you were ready to do something, but you were wrong. You ended up needing help after all. That's happened to me more than once. Tell an age-appropriate story from your own life. Then tell the kids it's their turn to tell their story to their partner and to listen as their partner shares a story too.

After kids share stories, ask for several volunteers to retell their stories—this time for the larger group. Say: **The disciples *did* have faith in Jesus. They'd watched what he could do and heard him teach. So how do you think they felt when Jesus told them they didn't have enough faith? That if they had faith the size of a mustard seed, they could move mountains?** Allow several kids to share their responses. Then give each child a mustard seed. Discuss:

- **How could something as small as a mustard seed move something as big as a mountain?**

- What do you think Jesus meant when he said that if his followers had faith as big as a mustard seed, nothing would be impossible?

Say: **When the disciples tried to help the boy, they made a mistake. They had faith in what** *they* **could do, not in what** *God* **could do. They relied on themselves rather than relying on God. Jesus wasn't saying to try harder to believe. He was telling his disciples—and us—to rely on God. So let's have faith in God!**

Give each child an envelope to put his or her mustard seed in and take home. Say: **Let your mustard seed be a reminder: With faith, nothing is impossible. Because with God, nothing is impossible!**

CLOSING PRAYER

LEANING ON JESUS

Time: about 5 minutes
Supplies: none

Have the kids line up side by side facing a wall. Ask them to move forward until they're standing just a few inches from the wall. They should put their hands out in front of them, palms against the wall, at chest height.

Say: **Please close your eyes as I lead us in prayer. God, thank you for always keeping your promises to us.** Now talk to the kids: **If you believe God keeps his promises, take a step away from the wall, but keep your hands where they are.** (pause as kids do this)

Pray: **Thank you, God, for loving us. If you believe God loves you, take another step away from the wall.** (pause) **Thank You, God, for our help, because with you, nothing is impossible. If you believe that with God nothing is impossible, take another step back, but keep leaning on the wall.** (pause)

God, thank you for always being trustworthy. If you trust God, take a step closer to the wall. (pause) **God, thank you for calling us your friends. If you are a friend of God or want to be, take a step closer to the wall.** (pause)

God, help us have faith in you, rely on you, lean on you, and be completely yours. If you'd like to lean or keep leaning on God, take a step closer to the wall. (pause) **Thank you, God. Amen.**

Say: **Having faith in and relying on God can be hard. He's as real as the wall you were leaning on, but you can't see him.**

EXTRA-TIME ACTIVITY–OPTION 1

WHO YOU GONNA TRUST?

Time: about 10 minutes
Supplies: none

Say: **It's easier to have faith in people when they tell us the truth and we know we can trust them. Sometimes people don't tell the truth—either because they lie or because they're just wrong. I'm going to say six things a lot of people say are true.** Ask the kids to stand up. **If you think something I say is false, sit down.** Read these one at a time, allowing kids time to respond before sharing whether the statement is true or false:

- **Tapping a soda can before opening it will keep it from foaming out, even if you've shaken the can.** (false)
- **In Rabbit Hash, Kentucky, a dog was elected mayor.** (true)
- **Eating carrots helps you see better.** (false)
- **Going outside with wet hair in the winter causes you to catch a cold.** (false)
- **Camels store water in their humps.** (false)
- **Christopher Columbus knew the world was round.** (true)
- **With faith, nothing is impossible.** (true)

Say: **God always tells the truth! That's one reason we can have faith in him!**

EXTRA-TIME ACTIVITY–OPTION 2

IMPOSSIBLE POSSIBILITIES

Time: about 5 minutes
Supplies: paper, pen

Gather the kids in a circle. Say: **Jesus told us that when we have faith in God, nothing is impossible. I'd like to pray for you over the next few** days, asking God to do something that improves what might feel like an impossible situation in your life.

Maybe your parents are fighting a lot, you have a bully you can't shake at school, or a friend of yours is seriously ill. Whatever it is, I'll ask God to work in the situation and in you. I believe God can do anything.

Be ready to write down what you're told. Letting kids see you take notes signals that you'll actually follow up and pray. If nobody speaks, look around expectantly and say nothing for at least 45 seconds. It will feel like an eternity, but it's time that kids may need to decide to risk speaking up.

Tuck your piece of paper into a pocket. Let kids know that they can come to you anytime with a prayer request. And perhaps it goes without saying, but do what you've promised. Pray, and pray often.

EXTRA-TIME ACTIVITY-OPTION 3

IMPOSSIBLE SNACK

Time: about 10 minutes
Supplies: individually wrapped candy (3 pieces per child), stopwatch

Give each child three pieces of candy, then ask the kids to put their candy on the floor in front of them. Say: **When I give you the word, feel free to eat your candy—but you can't use your hands to unwrap your candy.**

If you pull off your shoes, you can use your toes to unwrap it. Or you can lean over, pick up the candy with your teeth, and chew through the wrapping—but that's a really bad idea.

Whatever you decide, you have sixty seconds to unwrap your candy without using your hands. Starting ... now!

When sixty seconds is up, ask kids to discuss: **How impossible did this seem to you? Why?**

Thank kids for sharing their thoughts and then say: **You may remember I said that you couldn't unwrap *your* candy with *your* hands. There was no rule against unwrapping *someone else's* candy and that person unwrapping yours. If we'd all helped one another with what seemed impossible, it would have been possible. When we have faith in God and rely on him, what's impossible can become possible. Have faith in God!**

Jesus Said ...

It's Hard for Rich People to Enter God's Kingdom

The Point: Keep your focus on God.
Scripture Connect: Luke 18:18–27

Supplies for all session 12 activities options: pennies, paper, stopwatch, dollar bill, empty soda can, chair, Bible, wastebasket, pencils

The Basics for Leaders

When a wealthy man asked Jesus how to inherit eternal life, it was a great question. And this man asked precisely the right person who gave a great answer. But Jesus's answer was one the wealthy man didn't want to hear: Jesus told him to get rid of his money and follow him.

The money wasn't evil, but it was a distraction. And in the end, the rich man couldn't do it—he couldn't see past his money to focus only on God.

In this session, you'll help your kids do what the wealthy man couldn't: keep their focus on God and follow Jesus.

OPENING ACTIVITY-OPTION 1

TELL ME THUMBTHING

Time: about 5 minutes, depending on attendance
Supplies: none

After the kids arrive, say: **When people like a movie, they sometimes give it a thumbs-up.** (demonstrate) **If they really like the movie, they give it two thumbs-up. If they dislike or really dislike the movie, they give it one or two thumbs-down.** (demonstrate)

Say: **Please rate how this past week has gone for you. Was it a one or two thumbs-up week? A one or two thumbs-down week? Or maybe you'd give it one thumbs-up and one thumbs-down—it was a good *and* bad week. Rate your week now.**

After kids rate their weeks, give them 30 seconds each to explain why they rated their weeks as they did. You'll go first, sharing a story that models the sort of brief, personal stories you hope kids will share too.

Children will express themselves more over time, and hearing their stories will help you adapt this session to make it even more relevant to your kids' lives.

OPENING ACTIVITY-OPTION 2

PENNY PINCHERS

Time: about 10 minutes
Supplies: pennies (3 per child), paper, stopwatch, dollar bill

Give each child three pennies and provide a flat, uncarpeted area to spin them. If the room is carpeted, a few pieces of paper can be laid on the floor in front of each child. Tell the kids that the goal is to get all three pennies spinning at once. Demonstrate how to do this and then tell them they'll have two minutes to accomplish this task. When a child makes that happen, the child should yell out, "Penny Pincher!" Tell the kids to get in position. Say: **Ready? Set? Go!**

Keep talking and counting down the time as the kids spin pennies. Walk around the room and, as you do so, stealthily place a dollar bill in an easy-to-see spot. Quietly say: **Here's a dollar for anyone who wants it.** Drop the comment in the midst of your frantic encouragement for kids to keep pennies spinning. When two minutes have passed, discuss:

- **What was hard about this activity?**
- **What would have made it easier?**

As kids watch, pick up the dollar and pocket it. Ask why nobody wanted it. Mention that you offered the dollar, but nobody took it. Say: **You were so busy focusing on pennies that you let something more valuable slip past you. That's sort of what happened to a guy we'll meet today. I'll tell you more about that after a game!**

Surprising Sayings Game

DRAGON CAVE

Time: about 15 minutes
Supplies: pennies, empty soda can, chair

If the kids did the Option 2 activity, ask them to return their pennies to you. Put several pennies into the empty soda can and rattle it. Place a chair in the middle of the room and lay the can on its side under the chair.

Explain that the can is actually a huge mound of gold and gems, and perched on the chair is a dragon who'll do anything to defend his treasure. The good news is the dragon can't see, so if a child can move the treasure without it making noise, that child can steal the treasure. Say: **I'm looking for a dragon. Who's up to defend the treasure?**

Have the volunteer sit on the chair. Tell the dragon: **I can't blindfold you, so I'm trusting you to keep your eyes closed at all times—starting now. If you think you hear a thief making off with your treasure, point directly at the thief without looking. You get to point only once.**

Have the rest of the kids form a circle about six feet from the chair. Tell them to raise their hands if they want to steal the treasure. Point at one child who'll then move quietly to the chair, try to snag the can, and return it to his or her spot in the circle without the dragon noticing. If a thief is caught, he or she becomes the dragon. Play several rounds. Discuss:

- **If there really was a treasure, how hard would you work to get it? What would you do with the money?**
- **What's something you own that you'd work hard to defend? Why is it so important to you?**

Say: **I feel sorry for the dragon. He sits alone in a cave and can't invite friends over because he's afraid they might snag a diamond. Keeping treasure safe gets in the way of so many things. Maybe that's why Jesus said something surprising about people who have lots of money. Let's hear what he had to say.**

Surprising Sayings **Bible Story**

MONEY TROUBLES

Time: about 20 minutes
Supplies: Bible, paper (1 sheet per child)

Recruit two volunteers—one to play Jesus and the other to play a rich man. Tell the rest of the kids they're witnesses, or people who see what happens and are interviewed later about what they saw. Ask the volunteers to silently act out the story.

Read Luke 18:18–27 aloud, pausing often so Jesus and the rich man can act out what you're describing. When you've finished reading, have Jesus and the rich man sit with the other kids. Then conduct interviews. Ask the following:

- Witnesses, what part of what you saw and heard did you find surprising?
- Jesus, you told the man to get rid of his money and come follow you. Why?
- Rich man, you didn't do what Jesus asked. Why?
- Witnesses, how much money does someone have to have for you to think of that person as rich?
- Rich man, if you had it all to do over again, would you make the same choice? Why or why not?

Say: **It's hard to focus on both money and God at the same time. It's not that money is a bad thing—we can use it to help others, honor God, and take care of ourselves and people we love. But focusing on money** *instead* **of God** *is* **a bad thing.**

Give each child a sheet of paper. Say, **If your blank sheet of paper was a zillion-dollar bill, you'd look at it closely. Do that: hold it with both hands right up against your nose so you can see every detail.** (pause as kids do that) **Keep your paper right where it is and also look at me.** (pause) **You can't do it because your money gets in the way.**

Say: **Jesus said it's hard for rich people to enter God's kingdom. That's true not because they're rich but because rich people sometimes care more about their money than God. Money doesn't have to get in the way. We can use money to help others and still focus on God. But if money gets in our way, we'll have to make a choice: Focus on God or focus on money? The rich man chose money, but I'll bet he wouldn't make the same choice again. Let's ask Jesus to help us keep our focus on God.**

CLOSING PRAYER

IN GOD WE TRUST

Time: about 2 minutes
Supplies: pennies (1 per child)

Give each child a penny. Say: **In America, the pennies say, "In God We Trust." Find on your penny where it says this and trace the words with a fingertip.** If you're not using American pennies, skip this step!

Have kids hold their pennies in their palms, heads up. **Please pray along with me. God, we want to be with you in your kingdom. Help us always trust you and always focus on you.**

Then tell kids to turn their pennies over so they're tails-side up. Say: **Please pray with me again. God, help us turn our backs on anything that gets in the way of focusing on you. Give us the courage to follow you no matter what. Amen.**

EXTRA-TIME ACTIVITY—OPTION 1

MONEY MADNESS

Time: about 10 minutes
Supplies: pennies, wastebasket

Ask the kids to form pairs and give each pair a penny. Place a wastebasket in the center of the room and position pairs around the outside perimeter of the room. Tell the kids that one person in each pair will tilt her head back until she's looking at the ceiling. Then she'll close her eyes and place a penny on her chin.

The second person in each pair will tell his penny-chinned partner how to get to the wastebasket, where she'll tip her head forward and try to drop the penny into the wastebasket. Sighted partners are not allowed to touch their pennied friends. Ask the kid in each pair who's got the longest shoelaces to put the penny on her chin. After the first round, have kids retrieve pennies and have partners switch roles and play again. Discuss: **Tell us about a time when you were "blinded by money" and wanted something so much that you didn't care what it cost. What was it and did you get it?**

Say: **One cure for being blinded by money is to focus instead on God. He'll help you know what to do with your money if you just keep your focus on God!**

EXTRA-TIME ACTIVITY–OPTION 2

BOOT CAMP MULTITASKING

Time: about 5 minutes
Supplies: none

Review and rehearse with the kids the familiar song "Jesus Loves Me." Tell the kids you'll ask them to sing it, but as they sing, they also need to listen to you. That's because you'll give them instructions about what else to do as they sing.

After starting the song, shout out **"Jumping Jacks!"** and encourage kids to do that as they sing. Several seconds later, shout out **"Hop on one foot!"** and later **"Keep hopping and clap as you sing!"**

After several times through the song, with you adding more actions, the kids will be exhausted—and confused. Then let them sit down. Discuss:

- **What made this activity challenging?**
- **How hard or easy was it for you to focus on doing more than one thing at a time?**
- **How is this activity like focusing on God and money at the same time?**

Say: **Jesus must have surprised the rich man with his demand that the man give up his money and follow Jesus. But Jesus was offering the man life—eternal life. That's the same thing Jesus offers us if we'll put** aside whatever is between us and following him! Keep your focus on God because that's how to have real life!

EXTRA-TIME ACTIVITY—OPTION 3

PENNY SKETCH

Time: about 10 minutes
Supplies: paper (1 sheet per child), pencils, pennies (1 per child)

Before diving into this activity, collect any pennies that you have given the kids. Distribute paper and pencils. Instruct the kids to draw two circles on their papers, one circle next to the other. The circles should be roughly four inches in diameter. Hold up an example to help kids visualize what you're asking them to do.

Say: **We've been looking at pennies closely today. And you've probably seen thousands of pennies in the past. Draw the front of a penny in one circle and the back of a penny in the other circle. Add as many details as you can.** Give kids several minutes to draw, then distribute pennies so they can compare their sketches with actual pennies. Ask them to see how many details they got right and how many they missed.

Say: **We see pennies all the time, but we seldom *really* see them. We're busy focusing on other things and miss the details. It's like that with God too. We sometimes don't focus on him and miss seeing him at work in our world and in ourselves. Let's stop and focus right now. Put down your pennies and papers.** Discuss:

- **What in this room reminds you of what God's doing in the world and in you?**
- **Why is it so hard to focus on God? What gets in your way besides money?**

Thank kids for sharing and then give each child a penny. Say: **Don't spend this penny. Put it where you'll see it at home and let it be a reminder to keep your focus on God!**

Jesus Said ...

Care Most about the Life to Come

The Point: You can be friends with Jesus forever.
Scripture Connect: John 3:16; 12:25; 1 John 5:13

Supplies for all session 13 activities options: name tag stickers, index cards, markers, pencils, wastebasket, old blankets (or sheets), chairs (easily moved folding chairs are preferable), stopwatch, 2 balloons

The Basics for Leaders

For many children, *heaven* is just a vague notion and *eternity* a concept that's beyond them. But moving someplace new is a part of many children's lives. They've done it a time or two and often experience anxiety when the moving van pulls up yet again. So telling them they'll one day head to heaven might create more worry than joy.

But moving someplace wonderful where a best friend is waiting for them? That's reassuring—and exactly what happens when we arrive in heaven.

Some in Jesus's world were surprised to hear him talk about eternal life. They either didn't believe in it or didn't believe Jesus could provide it.

Today you'll help kids discover this wonderful truth: Jesus is life, and through him, his followers can experience eternal life. They have a friend in Jesus, and they can be friends with him forever.

OPENING ACTIVITY-OPTION 1

TELL ME THUMBTHING

Time: about 5 minutes, depending on attendance
Supplies: none

After the kids arrive, say: **When people like a movie, they sometimes give it a thumbs-up.** (demonstrate) **If they really like the movie, they give it two thumbs-up. If they dislike or really dislike the movie, they give it one or two thumbs-down.** (demonstrate)

Say: **Please rate how this past week has gone for you. Was it a one or two thumbs-up week? A one or two thumbs-down week? Or maybe you'd give it one thumbs-up and one thumbs-down—it was a good** *and* **bad week. Rate your week now.**

After kids rate their weeks, give them 30 seconds each to explain why they rated their weeks as they did. You'll go first, sharing a story that models the sort of brief, personal stories you hope kids will share too.

Children will express themselves more over time, and hearing their stories will help you adapt this session to make it even more relevant to your kids' lives.

OPENING ACTIVITY-OPTION 2

IT'S ALWAYS SOMETHING

Time: about 10 minutes
Supplies: none

Say: **I'm going to tell you about four places, and you'll decide which one sounds like someplace you'd like to live forever.** Explain that you'll tell the kids about a danger in each place and what to do if they encounter it. They'll vote on whether your advice is good or bad.

Say: **In Colorado, you're caught in a sudden avalanche. My advice? Try to outrun it by dashing downhill before the snow reaches you.** Put this advice to a vote, then explain: **This is** *terrible* **advice, because you can't outrun an avalanche.**

Say: **In Arizona:, you just got bit by a rattlesnake. My advice? Use a knife to cut around the bite and suck out the venom.** Put this advice to a vote, then explain: **Nope. Cutting the bite just adds a knife wound to the bite problem.**

Say: **In California, you come across a black bear, and he's not happy. My advice? Get close and rub his muzzle so he falls asleep.** Put this advice to a vote, then explain: **No! Better to stand your ground, avoid eye contact, slowly back away, and make yourself as big as possible.**

Say: **In heaven, you can live with Jesus forever. My advice? Love and follow Jesus so you can go to heaven. And there's nothing wrong about this place. It's perfect!**

Say: **You have four choices: Colorado, Arizona, California, or heaven.** Read the list again and give the kids time to raise their hands for where they'd like to live forever. Say: **Jesus said we're built to live for eternity. The question is, where will we spend eternity? Jesus wants us to be with him in heaven, where we'll be friends with him forever. We'll talk more about that after a quick game.**

Surprising Sayings Game

WHOOZIT?

Time: about 15 minutes
Supplies: name tag stickers, index cards, markers, empty wastebasket

Before the kids arrive, prepare an index card and place it in the wastebasket. On the card, write these three words: *friend, forever,* and *family.* Fill out a card about yourself too, following the directions you'll give kids.

Give each child a name tag sticker, an index card, and a marker. Say: **When making new friends, it helps to know something about them. And even if you're already friends, there's still a lot to learn.**

Tell the kids to fill out their name tag stickers, but instead of writing their real names, tell them to create new names. For their first names, they'll write the name of their first pet. If they've never had a pet, they can use a fun, made-up name. For their last names, they'll write the name of the street where they live. When finished, kids can peel off the backs of the stickers and wear their name tags.

Say: **You'll now fill out your card, but what you write is top secret.** Ask the kids to write three things on the front of their cards: their favorite color, their favorite superhero, and their favorite ice cream flavor. **On the back of your card, write three words that describe you.** Once the kids have finished writing, walk around with the empty wastebasket and collect cards. Ask the kids to sit in a circle. When reading the cards, do so in the wastebasket so handwriting doesn't give away who wrote which card.

Say: **Let's see how well we know one another. Who wrote this?** Read aloud one or two of the words from the front of a card and one or two things from the back of the card. Let kids guess who it is and call out the new names that are on name tags. Make sure that every child is highlighted at least once.

Then read the card you prepared. See if anyone can guess who you're describing. Say: **It's Jesus! And because he said that where even a few of his followers are together, he's there also, I know he's here in our circle with us.** Ask: **In what ways do those three words—*friend*, *forever*, and *family*—describe Jesus?**

Say: **Jesus got in a lot of trouble with some people when he said something surprising about being a friend forever. Let's hear what he said and what was said about him.**

Surprising Sayings **Bible Story**

FOREVER TOGETHER

Time: about 15 minutes
Supplies: Bible, old blankets (or sheets), chairs (easily moved folding chairs are preferable), stopwatch

Say: **In the next five minutes, you are to work together to build a covered shelter we can all fit inside. Use these blankets and the furniture in the room. Get building!** Allow time for the kids to build. Add some urgency by counting down the time and asking kids to check and double-check that everyone will fit under the shelter. Once the shelter is complete, join kids in it and congratulate them for their work.

Say: **This is a temporary shelter. The buildings where you live are far stronger, but they're temporary too. Sooner or later, those buildings will wear out and be torn down. But there's a permanent place that will last forever. It's heaven, and here's the good news: Jesus wants you to join him there. You can do that when you accept Jesus as your Savior. You can be friends with Jesus forever!**

That's what Jesus said, and it's what some Bible writers said too. Ask a willing child to read John 3:16 aloud. No volunteers? You can read the passage aloud yourself. Explain that while we may be used to hearing those words from Jesus, many people who heard him say things like this were surprised. Why? Because Jesus was saying that he's the way to God. That's a big claim!

Say: **And Jesus was saying there's eternal life. Some Jewish religious leaders—the Sadducees—didn't believe in an afterlife. Jesus was not only disagreeing with them; he was claiming to be the key to that afterlife. Let's hear something else Jesus said.**

Ask a volunteer to read John 12:25 aloud. Say: **And one of the Bible writers wrote this.** Ask a volunteer to read 1 John 5:13 aloud. **Jesus made it very clear: there is eternal life, and we can be his friends forever.** Discuss:

- How do you feel knowing that Jesus wants you as his forever friend? Why?
- Most of us don't think about heaven very much, even though we'll spend a lot of time there. Why don't we think more about it?
- What questions do you have about heaven?

After the discussion, ask the kids to join you outside the shelter. Say: **Be careful getting out—we don't want to have our shelter fall down just yet!**

CLOSING PRAYER

PREPARING FOR THE MOVE
Time: about 5 minutes
Supplies: none

Say: **We scrambled to set up the shelter. But a time is coming when there won't be any need to hurry because we'll be in heaven with Jesus forever. I look forward to heaven and being with Jesus. And to being with Jesus's other friends—including you! When you believe in Jesus and accept him as your Lord and Savior, you'll be friends with Jesus forever.**

Ask the kids to carefully and slowly fold up the blankets and put the furniture back in place. As they do so, ask them to say aloud words that describe Jesus. As they work together, encourage them to keep saying words that describe Jesus. Once they're done, say: **Since Jesus is with us all the time, he's heard what you said about him. So this has been our prayer. Amen.**

EXTRA-TIME ACTIVITY–OPTION 1

FANCY FRIENDS HANDSHAKE

Time: about 5 minutes
Supplies: none

Ask the kids to each find a partner. As needed, you can join the fun! Say: **Sometimes friends create special handshakes. You and your partner have a few minutes to create your own fancy handshake. Use fist bumps, high fives, hand slaps, finger snaps, or whatever's fun.**

The challenge is making up something you can remember because you'll show your handshakes to the rest of us. Ready? Go! Allow a few minutes for the kids to create their special handshakes, then have pairs demonstrate for the larger group. Applaud all efforts.

Say: **It's great to have friends, but it's even better to have forever friends. That's what we have in Jesus—a forever friend. We can be friends with Jesus forever!**

EXTRA-TIME ACTIVITY–OPTION 2

FIRE!

Time: about 10 minutes
Supplies: none

Ask the kids to picture themselves at home. They smell smoke. Say: **If this really happened, the best thing you could do would be to make sure everyone knew there was a fire so you could all get out safely.**

But in our imaginary fire, everyone's already out the door. Everything alive is already safe. Everything you own is between you and the door, so you have time to scoop up two things to take with you. What two things would you grab and why? Turn to a neighbor and talk about that.

Allow the kids time to talk and then ask them to report what they discussed with the whole group. After the kids have shared, say: **When you go to heaven, you don't get to take anything with you. It's just you—nothing else. In what ways does knowing you can't take anything with you change how you feel about being in heaven forever? Or doesn't it? Why?**

Say: **I don't think I'll miss my childhood teddy bear once I get to heaven. Being friends with Jesus forever will more than make up for** leaving my little bear behind. I'm glad Jesus is my friend now and will be my friend forever!

EXTRA-TIME ACTIVITY–OPTION 3

BALLOON BOP

Time: about 10 minutes
Supplies: 2 inflated balloons, wastebasket

Place a wastebasket at one end of the room and gather the kids at the other end. Explain that the goal of this game is to keep the balloon in the air by bopping it upward as they move the balloon across the room and into the wastebasket.

> **TIP**
>
> If the kids stay in single file, rotating to the back of the line as they move across the room, they won't get in each other's way.

Explain the rules:

1. No one can move the wastebasket.
2. No one can touch the balloon twice until everyone has bopped it once, and no one can bop it a third time until everyone has bopped it twice.
3. If the balloon hits the floor, you must start over from the beginning.

You've got to work together as friends for this to work. Ready? Let's go!

Walk alongside the kids, helping them get and stay organized. Once the balloon's in the wastebasket, try it again with two balloons, using the same rules. After playing, discuss:

- How was this game like how friendships work?
- What made it easier or harder to get organized and move the balloon?

Say: I love doing things with friends! That's one reason I'm excited about the life to come in heaven: I'll be with friends ... forever! And one friend I have now who'll be waiting for me there is Jesus. We can be friends with Jesus forever!

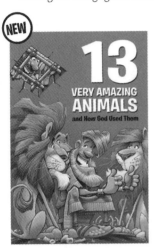

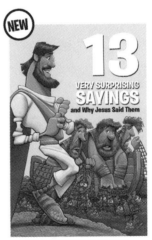